ROAD TRANSPORT MANAGEMENT AND ACCOUNTING

R. G. BASSETT
F.C.M.A., A.C.I.S.

Management Development Adviser,
Road Transport Industry Training Board

HEINEMANN : LONDON

William Heinemann Ltd

15 Queen St. Mayfair, London W1X 8BE

LONDON   MELBOURNE   TORONTO

JOHANNESBURG   AUCKLAND

$$\frac{A}{658.91}$$

Text set in 10/12 pt Monotype Times New Roman
printed by letterpress and bound in Great Britain by
Butler & Tanner Ltd, Frome and London

TO MARY

Editor's Foreword

The Heinemann Accountancy and Administration Series is intended to fill a gap in the literature that caters for accountants, company secretaries, and similar professional people who are engaged in giving a vital information service to management. As far as possible, due recognition is given to the fact that there are two distinct bodies of readers: those who aspire to professional status – the students – and others who are already managing or serving management.

The road transport industry now plays an important role in the economy of the country. It provides an essential link between the provider of goods and the users.

Because of the competitive nature of the industry, there is need for effective management and an awareness of the consequences of decisions on the financial position. There should be planning, control, and co-ordination of the various functions. This may be achieved through budgetary control, standard costing, and related costing techniques. The overall profitability and solvency may be watched and monitored by the employment of accounting ratios.

This book covers the essentials of road transport management and accounting. It examines the principles and applications. Written by R. G. Bassett, an expert on Management Development in the Road Transport Industry, the practical approach adopted is certain to appeal to the practising manager and accountant. Students will also find the concise presentation readily lends itself to assimilation and understanding.

J. BATTY

Preface

This book has been specially written for managers and other personnel who are engaged in road transport activities, firstly to meet an ever-growing demand for managerial-control information in freight transport undertakings, and secondly to fill a gap that has existed for far too long.

Because transport managers and other officials are busy people, the book has been written in simple, everyday terms, starting with basic road transport management and ending with financial aspects of business planning. It is assumed that the reader has no prior knowledge of costing or accounting, and for that reason no apology is given for the elementary way in which the subject matter is presented. All illustrations and figures have been geared to road transport operations. A suggested reading list is included at the end of the book for those readers who wish to pursue the matter further.

The object of the book is therefore to give managers in freight transport an appreciation of the methods and techniques available which are a prerequisite to decision making, planning, and control. It is also hoped that costing and accounting personnel in road transport undertakings will find the book helpful in the performance of their daily tasks; and that students studying for professional and degree examinations with a transport bias will find the text of invaluable assistance when preparing for the various accounting papers.

Last, but not least, the book will be of value to college lecturers, teachers, accountants, and training officers who are responsible for transport courses and require an easy reference guide covering the various aspects of road transport management and accounting; and to accountants (and consultants) in public practice who need to advise their clients more specifically on transport matters.

Rochester, Kent   R. G. BASSETT

Contents

PART THREE – FINANCIAL PLANNING AND
CONTROL

Introduction—
The Road Transport Problem

0.1 THE ROAD TRANSPORT INDUSTRY

Road transport – the carriage of goods by road vehicles – is a vast and grow-ing industry. Of all the modes of inland freight transport in the United Kingdom (rail, air, waterways, etc.) road transport handles the largest volume of traffic in terms of weight-distance. The latter was 55 per cent of all freight transport in 1962, 59 per cent in 1964, 61 per cent in 1966 (*The Transport of Freight*, Cmnd 3470, HMSO, 1967), and about 63 per cent in 1972 (*Annual Abstract of Statistics* 1972 No. 109, C.S.O., HMSO). The current opinion is that the percentage is still climbing.

In terms of expenditure it is stated that £2,720 million was spent on road freight transport in 1969, excluding the net investment in new vehicles estimated at £450 million (*Highway Statistics* 1969, Ministry of Transport, HMSO, 1970). If only 1 per cent of the total expenditure could be saved through more effective management the annual saving could be something approaching £32 million.

That is what this book is about.

0.2 THE TRANSPORT MANAGER

Hitherto road transport management has been a sadly neglected subject, while marketing, production, finance, and personnel management have had their fair share of attention. The tide has turned, however, since it was realized that vast cost savings can be made from an efficient transport system; and the transport manager, who until comparatively recently was probably the most underrated manager in the business world, can now face his industrial and commercial counterparts with complete confidence, knowing that his job is just as vital as theirs, and that their training needs are no different from his.

0.3 THE DISTRIBUTION SYSTEM

Distribution of freight by road consists of three main activities:

1 Trunking bulk freight from supply points (e.g. factories, ports, warehouses) to distribution centres.
2 Off-loading, storing, and the breaking of bulk.
3 Delivery to customer points from distribution centres.

The 'total cost function' is therefore made up of trunking, depot, and delivery costs. ('Depot' here is taken to mean the warehouse, branch, etc., where goods are stored, sorted, etc.) Moreover, goods can be trunked and delivered by either own-account or haulage operators or both.

The object of this book is therefore to determine ways and means of reducing the total cost function so that transport operators stand to gain, and, indeed, the economy as a whole.

0.4 ROAD TRANSPORT MANAGEMENT

Freight management is therefore seen as one gigantic cost problem. For that reason it is essential to tackle the problem correctly, starting with road transport management. There is little point in costing fleet operations, for example, unless the fleet has been properly organized and is being effectively managed. It is necessary to ensure that the fleet is of the right size. Too many operators today are using too many vehicles because their routeing system (if they have one) is inadequate. Routeing is no easy task, however, because of the large number of variables that affect it (e.g. the number of collection/delivery points, time, distance, drops). Just as cost savings in manufacturing begin at the design/production-planning stage, so cost savings in road transport begin at the vehicle design/fleet-planning stage.

Then there is the way in which the transport manager handles the various aspects of his job. Unless he is objective in dealing with people and the situations that arise daily he may not achieve the goals so vital to prosperity and growth. Of course, his objectives must first be defined and agreed and should stem from the overall business plan. If no plan exists then the manager – and indeed the company or department – is in a very precarious position. Management by objectives is therefore a most vital factor in transport operations.

0.5 HAULIER *v.* OWN-ACCOUNT OPERATOR

The point to bear in mind throughout this book is that haulage and own-account operations are not so very different, if at all. Both are concerned with the transportation of freight from A to B in the most effective manner; and both are equally concerned with cost control. At the same time, they each have their own peculiar problems. The haulier, for instance, has to market his services and employ realistic traffic rates; sometimes he may subcontract work or hire additional vehicles. The own-account operator sometimes has a capacity problem because of market changes (e.g. product innovation and geographical demand), and may therefore resort to vehicle hire or the employment of contract services. If either operator decided to acquire new or additional vehicles he would most certainly consider the same cost factors.

0.6 THE 'PROFIT' MOTIVE

The real difference between the haulier and the own-account operator is said to be that of profit: the haulier carries for hire and reward whereas the own-account operator carries the company's own goods without apparent reward. However, it would be foolish indeed to assume that own-account operators are not interested in the profit motive. Profit is just as important to them as it is to hauliers, but it is more obvious in the latter case.

There are three aspects of own-account 'profit' to consider, namely, cost savings, economic profit, and actual profit.

0.6.1 COST SAVINGS

The importance of cost control in private transport is no different from that in haulage operations. By minimizing transport costs company profit is enhanced. An annual saving of, say, £5,000 would increase profit by the same amount. This simple illustration is sufficient to underline the fact that private-transport managers *are* motivated by the profit factor in terms of cost savings.

0.6.2 ECONOMIC PROFIT

The 'economic profit' is the difference between the own-account operator's minimum operating costs at maximum efficiency (*or* actual costs) and the cost of outside transport services (i.e. using contract services instead of company vehicles), i.e.

External-transport costs
less Own-transport costs
Economic profit

External-transport costs can be obtained by taking the weight-distance (or other) factors for the selected period and quantifying them at the average external rate. The resultant economic profit would show whether or not the investment in the company's fleet was earning an adequate return. If, for example, the economic profit was £10,000 and the average investment £50,000, the return of 20 per cent would be considered satisfactory.

0.6.3 ACTUAL PROFIT

The actual profit would be the difference between the company's total annual transport operating costs (which could be anything above the minimum costs possible at maximum operating efficiency) and the total annual transport charges contained within the price of the commodity.

Although most manufacturers include transport costs in their unit prices (perhaps by using 'average' costs because of geographical factors) and employ their own distribution service, it would appear that not all bother to determine the profit or loss arising from the operation. This applies equally to companies which make a separate charge for their transport services.

Own-account transport profit can be expressed simply thus:

Transport revenue or charges
less Transport operating costs
Profit or loss

It should be remembered that where operating costs are minimized company profit is maximized.

0.6.4 OWN-ACCOUNT OPERATORS AND PROFIT

A number of own-account operators have organized their transport function into a separate limited company, charge out their services at selected traffic rates, and show a 'profit' at the end of the trading year. Many transport departments adopt a similar procedure and produce 'profit and loss' accounts on a regular basis.

It is therefore emphasized that the profit motive stressed throughout the book does not necessarily apply to hauliers only, even though haulage operations are frequently mentioned. The profit motive is very much a part of own-account transport policy, and woe betide the transport manager who thinks otherwise.

0.7 HOW THE BOOK HAS BEEN ARRANGED

Having stressed the fact that the haulier and the own-account operator are no different and that profit enhancement through effective cost control is their common aim, together with an efficient and reliable transport service, we can proceed to the main body of the book. The book has been arranged in three parts.

0.7.1   PART ONE

Part One deals with important aspects of road transport management. Unless transport management is properly structured, organized, and follows an objective policy, there can be little hope of effective cost control. Management is concerned with matters other than cost control, however, such as marketing, driver and vehicle management, fleet planning, and so on, although each will impinge in some way on the cost and profit situation.

Chapter 1 outlines the importance of establishing the transport manager's place in the management structure and in defining his authority, activities, and those objectives for which he is personally responsible. That surely is the starting point. This is followed by discussion of a number of important matters which the manager must deal with, or be aware of, if he is to be effective in his job. They include customer marketing, vehicle and driver management (including vehicle maintenance, replacement, and load requirements), insurance and legal considerations, and the need to adopt the management-by-objectives approach. 'Padding' has been avoided and only the basic essentials are stated.

Chapter 2 deals with a matter which is often taken for granted: fleet size. A general discussion of the factors affecting fleet size is given, as this is an essential part of fleet management and the starting point for cost control. It should be every operator's aim to maximize the return on the minimum fleet investment, by restricting the fleet to a realistic size and utilizing it to the full, especially in an age when drivers are in short supply.

Chapter 3 is a natural follow-on from Chapter 2 as it deals with the various problems of vehicle routeing and depot siting. The object of fleet size appraisal is to save *vehicles*, whereas the object of vehicle routeing and depot siting is to save *kilometres*. Both vehicles and kilometres saved have an important bearing on a company's profit and cash flow position and should therefore be regarded with the utmost objectivity.

0.7.2   PART TWO

Part Two deals with the costing and pricing of fleet operations. The various chapters cover why costing is necessary, its relationship with estimating (or price fixing), what road transport costs are and from what sources they arise, overheads and their recovery, workshop costing, and so on.

Chapter 9 deals specifically with a typical costing system which could be used in practice.

Chapter 10 deals with the important subject of rate fixing and profit.

0.7.3   PART THREE

Part Three deals with various aspects of financial planning and control in a road transport situation. Budgetary control and standard costing are basic essentials of any control system and are therefore given some attention in Chapters 11 and 12.

Chapter 13 defines break-even analysis and marginal costing and illustrates their importance in decision making and profit planning.

Ways of replacing vehicles are described in Chapter 14 which stresses the importance of using comparative-cost tables.

Capital investment appraisal, dealt with in Chapter 15, is nothing new, but discounted cash flow has now replaced (or absorbed) some of the older methods and should be understood by every transport manager.

Chapter 16 deals with the importance of management ratios in terms of profitability and liquidity, which must go hand in glove if survival, prosperity, and growth are to be attained.

Finally, Chapter 17 looks at the financial aspects of business long-range planning.

Part One

ROAD TRANSPORT MANAGEMENT

1 The Transport Manager and His Job

1.1 MANAGEMENT JOB DESCRIPTIONS

Until comparatively recently the transport manager was probably the most underrated manager in the business world. Usually he was placed at the end of the management line, after marketing, production, financial, and personnel management. Often he was regarded as a sort of ex-driver type of individual, who readily understood vehicles but knew little about management techniques and methods.

While it is true that transport management has been a sadly neglected subject in the past, the matter has now taken a turn in the transport manager's favour. The vast cost savings and operating potential to be derived from an efficient transport system is now uppermost in people's minds, and distributors, employers' associations, consultants, and academics are now paying this age-old industry a good deal of attention. It goes without saying that without an efficient road transport system the national economy would come to a grinding halt.

The role of the transport manager has therefore taken on a new perspective. Everything is now being done to further his development in management matters. It should be noted, however, that the transport manager's training needs (in, say, operating, financial, and personnel matters) are no different from those of his counterparts in other industries.

Although the transport manager's job may vary from company to company a good deal of his work will nevertheless remain constant (e.g. driver and vehicle management, cost control, maintenance, routeing, scheduling) because these are essentially transport matters. Even so it is important that, following good management practice, the manager's job should be clearly defined on paper.

Management job descriptions, so rightly advocated by the Road Transport Industry Training Board, ensure that each manager is aware of the fundamentals of his job: its purpose, to whom he reports and those who report to him, other staff and line relationships, his limits of authority, his key tasks or duties, and, most important of all, the precise goals and targets for which he is personally responsible – for it is by their achievement that efficiency and profitability are attained.

It is an axiom that no two managers can be responsible for the same tasks. The compilation of job descriptions very often brings to light duplication of effort, and sometimes leads to a complete revision of the management structure.

Once a manager's job has been defined and agreed and his job description drawn up, it need only be revised if and when important changes take place, but certainly annually if his quantified goals and targets are contained therein. It should therefore be geared to the company's financial or trading year.

The main areas of a management job description might therefore appear as follows:

Example:

Management Job Description

Name of job holder:_____   Job title: Transport Manager

Applicable from: _____   to:_____

1 *Main purpose of job*

(e.g. '. . . to provide effective overall control of fleet activities and the attainment of the goals and objectives as defined in the fleet operating budget and supporting schedules.')

2 *Position in organization*

Reports to: (e.g. general manager)
Immediate subordinates: (specific job positions – not surnames)
Functional relationships: (internal and external relationships necessary for the performance of duties)

3 *Job resources*

(i.e. the resources within the manager's charge which he must use to produce results)
Personnel: (the total staff within the manager's control)
Vehicles: (number, type, and class)
Facilities: (e.g. workshops, yard space, office)

4 *Personnel activities*

(i.e. those activities which are the direct responsibility of the manager and which cannot be delegated. They should be listed in order of importance.)

5 *Limits of authority*

(e.g. capital expenditure, petty-cash expenditure, operating expenditure, the engagement and dismissal of staff, overtime authorization, changing policies and established procedures. Each item should be quantified to be effective.)

6 *Major responsibilities for results*

(This is the focal point of the job description. It specifies – or refers to the documents which contain – the quantified targets, goals, or objectives which the manager must achieve over the agreed operating period (week, month, quarter, or year). Examples are: fleet utilization, weight–distance targets, turnover, expenditure controls, profit, reduction in staff turnover (e.g. drivers), new business, maintenance programmes, breakdown minimization, reduction in fleet size by a given date without a fall-off in the traffic carried. The use of ratios, percentages, figures, dates, and times are therefore preferable to subjective phrases such as 'maximum', 'satisfactory', 'reasonable', 'adequate', etc. The former can be measured for appraisal purposes; the latter cannot.)

Once each manager's job description has been drawn up and agreed it should be signed by the job holder. The various job descriptions should support every position on the management tree.

The chief executive will know with assurance that each managerial position is both meaningful and objective, that there are no overlaps, and that each manager – by achieving his objectives – is contributing to the company's/department's overall business objectives.

The performance appraisal of each manager by his immediate superior on a regular basis cannot be overstressed if his motivation and development are to be encouraged. Besides discussing whether or not the manager achieved his agreed objectives, and the reasons why he did or did not (taking into account the controllable and uncontrollable elements), the appraiser should also take into account the attitude he displays to his work and to those with whom he works, as well as his own views on his career development.

1.2 MARKETING

Because the business climate is frequently changing, operators need to be constantly on their guard against the effect of change on their future operations. The advent of the container is a typical example; when introduced it left many operators with empty vehicles. Until fairly recently the average distributor/haulier has not taken the marketing function very seriously, but changing conditions are compelling him to take a broader view of the business situation. Change can be detected by market trend analysis, either through the marketing department or by using market research agencies.

In most cases innovation is brought about by:

1 Product changes, price, and volume.
2 Changes in retail practices (e.g. the growth of supermarkets, cash-and-carry outlets, mail order stores, etc.).
3 Sociological changes and the demand for variety.
4 Technological changes (e.g. the freight-liner, Ro-Ro ferry services, air freighting).
5 Government intervention (e.g. the various road traffic orders and regulations affecting vehicles, drivers, loads, speed, etc.).
6 Management techniques in problem solving and business competition which are becoming more and more profound.

Although the items listed are a mixture of marketing and business development considerations they are nevertheless closely interlinked in that the transport operator must gear his services to meet each of them, as it arises, at the lowest possible cost. In other words, the operator must continually aim to meet the changing needs of his customers if he is to continue to serve them.

At this point it is important to stress that there are two aspects of marketing to consider. The first concerns the own-account operator and the company's goods he carries. Marketing in this sense is primarily concerned with the company's products in meeting the needs of the user. Of necessity this must include a reliable, speedy, and efficient distribution service (the cost of which would be built into the product price). The distribution function is therefore an essential part of marketing and involves at the outset careful liaison with the marketing and production departments. Similarly the haulier will require to know the precise needs of his clients (manufacturer, wholesaler, etc.) if he is to meet them by effective vehicle scheduling.

The second aspect of marketing is that both operators need to market their own services (the haulier in particular) for meeting department, company, or customer requirements. Many manufacturers have their own transport companies (e.g. S.P.D. Ltd, Reed Transport Ltd) and cannot afford to wait for work to come to them. Like the haulier they must go after traffic through an effective marketing strategy, as they too will very likely be competing with other operators.

The importance of determining customers' needs cannot be over-emphasized; it is the basis for sound marketing practice. A number of operators may dismiss the idea by stating either that they are 'too small' for the practice to apply to them, or that they cannot afford the time or expense to devote to it – in short, that their future does not matter. The wise operator will, however, tap the vast resource at his fingertips by analysing his customers' real needs both present and future in terms of quantity, weight, location, distance, seasonality, equipment needs, special requirements, and so on.

There are two ways in which this can be effected:

1 By analysing existing customer data (e.g. invoices, dispatch records, bills of lading, customer records) and discussing with customers their future needs.
2 By means of a confidential customer questionnaire delivered through the post or by personal call (e.g. by sales representatives). If the former it should not be sent without some prior warning, or it might finish up in the wastepaper basket.

The analysis of customers' requirements could also be undertaken by a market research agency, though at a price.

The analysis would very likely reveal that most customers have different requirements, each of which represents a piece of the jigsaw which an operator has to piece together to formulate his business strategy. Opportunity should also be taken of determining customers' strengths and weaknesses in terms of public image, financial structure, expansionist policies, and the like, all of which should be noted on a customer analysis record, as these considerations may well affect the operator's own growth plans in due course. Customer requirements could include the need for facilities such as special storage (e.g. cold storage), additional geographical location points, special packaging devices, a returnable container service, special loading equipment, special delivery requirements (e.g. at night), cash-on-delivery services, and so on, all of which must be carefully considered by the operator in terms of resource planning (i.e. cash, vehicles, depots, etc.). By expressing customer requirements in terms of weight (or volume) and delivery times over a selected time scale the operator would know whether or not his fleet capacity was adequate.

If a questionnaire is used it should be drawn up by the marketing team (or the person responsible for that function which, in a small firm, could be the transport manager), having regard to all the relevant commercial and operating factors. The Sales Council of the American Trucking Association, in its 'Guide for Effective Marketing and Sales Management' series, lists twenty customer items for its members to consider, ranging from merchandising practices (i.e. channels of distribution, outlets, and selling practices) to profit opportunities. Detailed knowledge of key customers is stressed, as is the mutual-profitability relationship between customer and operator.

Marketing is therefore an essential part of road transport management. Unless operators determine their customers' needs and organize their businesses to meet them – because that is what marketing is all about, the meeting of a need at an economic price – their future may well be in jeopardy. By helping companies to improve their distribution systems the transport operator is safeguarding his own interests and will build up a favourable image and future.

1.3 VEHICLE MANAGEMENT

Goods vehicles should be of the right shape and size (i.e. type and capacity) and of the right number and mix; they should be clean, well maintained, and replaced at the right time. The way in which they are acquired is also part of vehicle management. The orders and regulations concerning motor vehicles must also be taken into account. Some of these items are dealt with further on (Chapters 2 and 14). The remaining items dealt with here – maintenance, replacement, vehicle legislation – are all closely interlinked.

1.3.1 VEHICLE MAINTENANCE

The degree of vehicle maintenance required depends upon a number of factors, among them: vehicle design and suitability to the job it performs; operating conditions, terrain, and climate; driving skills; maintenance policy; and the comparatively new regulations concerning vehicle roadworthiness.

The transport manager should satisfy himself that his vehicles are roadworthy when they leave the yard, even though this may be the prime responsibility of the fleet engineer. The fact that poorly maintained vehicles can kill, incur the operator in heavy fines, and upset the scheduling routine are reasons enough for effective management in this area. The transport manager and fleet engineer have an unwritten responsibility to the company, customer, driver, the public at large, and indeed the law to maintain the fleet in effective working order.

A maintenance policy is the best way of controlling the maintenance problem. Like most policies it should be in writing, specify the procedure and format to be adopted, and assign responsibility. The format should include a 'maintenance schedule' whereby vehicles undergo regular inspection checks and routine maintenance at selected intervals. The maintenance interval should take into account operating conditions including 'mileage'; different vehicles would probably have different intervals. The maintenance schedule should specify all the points to be covered during the maintenance process, each of which should be signed by the fitter on completion.

Roving inspections and drivers' reports on vehicle defects enhance good maintenance practice. Weekly checks on oil and battery levels, lighting, wheel nuts, etc., are over and above general maintenance and should be the responsibility of the driver. The need to clean the underside of a vehicle for the maintenance/inspection routine is important.

Once the maintenance schedule has been drawn up and agreed the transport manager will know from his copy when certain vehicles are required by the workshop (and indeed when certain vehicles should be returned), and will thus be able to plan for the contingency well in advance.

Maintenance costing and workshop cost control are dealt with in Chapters 6 and 8.

1.3.2 VEHICLE REPLACEMENT

Although vehicles will run for ever if properly maintained there are very good reasons for replacing them at certain intervals. The first reason is the escalation in maintenance costs as a vehicle gets older (and the difficulty of obtaining parts); the second reason is the need to invest in more modern vehicles to enhance operating efficiency and preserve the company image; the third reason is changes in business activity (i.e. customers requiring special-purpose vehicles); and the fourth reason is that it is better to invest in new vehicles than spend the same money on old vehicles by way of repair and maintenance.

When should vehicles be replaced? The answer depends upon company policy and any or all of the reasons noted above. The availability of funds also comes into it, especially if the company's policy is to buy outright. Many operators adopt the visual-inspection approach in conjunction with the recorded maintenance costs to date and the fleet engineer's report. Others fix replacement dates based on past experience with the type of vehicle being considered, perhaps extending the period when funds are tight.

Some operators are known to base their replacement policy on 'plant replacement' theory, which takes into account capital, maintenance, and depreciation costs and ignores those costs which do not change (i.e. running costs).

Note: In the example overleaf the depreciation charges are based on the estimated fall in market value of the vehicle, so that at the end of seven years the resale value would be something of the order of £700. This figure is not unduly high when we consider the large repair bills over the last two years needed to put the vehicle in good working order.

Example:

The following figures relate to a vehicle with a capital cost of £3,000:

Age (years)	Maintenance £	Depreciation £	Total £	Cumulative £	Average £
0–1	50	900	950	950	950
1–2	170	600	770	1,720	860
2–3	300	400	700	2,420	807
3–4	430	200	630	3,050	762
4–5	640	100	740	3,790	758
5–6	760	50	810	4,600	766
6–7	800	50	850	5,450	779

The table tells us that the time to replace the vehicle is when the average annual cost is at its lowest, in this case at the end of the fifth year when the market value is about £800. The table can be extended by introducing other important features such as tax allowances, corporation tax, and discounting.

It is considered dangerous practice to replace a vehicle when a certain point in a table has been reached. For one thing the estimates contained in the table could be wrong; for another, circumstances may not require another vehicle of that particular type, or the cash position may not support it. A sound replacement policy must therefore take all relevant factors into account, and the authority to purchase should be geared to a capital expenditure programme such as that described in Chapter 11.

1.3.3 VEHICLE LEGISLATION

The fact that selected goods vehicles with an unladen weight of over 1,525 kg (kilograms), and trailers of over 1,020 kg, must be tested annually at one of the D.o.E. test stations is reason enough to maintain vehicles in good working order. The test is conducted in accordance with the *Goods Vehicle Testers' Manual* and covers at present sixty-four items ranging from the position of the legal plate to maintenance of the parking brake. Failure to pass the test can upset operating schedules, but minor faults can be put right during the test providing a fitter accompanies the vehicle to the test station.

Operators' vehicles have always been maintained in one form or another – either in their own workshops or by outside contractors – but the new legislation requires higher maintenance quality control if the stringent test criteria are to be met. Operators who subcontract repair work to garages should remember that they are still responsible for the condition of their vehicles, even though defects may be the result of ineffective workmanship at the garage.

Inspection checks as part of maintenance policy has already been touched upon (section 1.3.1). Also, they are required by legislation (Road Safety Act 1968, section 18). Operating conditions and 'mileage' determine how often a vehicle should be inspected. Companies which do not have their own workshop can employ specialist services such as the Freight Transport Association's 'Quality Control Maintenance Inspection Service', the Ford Motor Company's 'Contract Confidence' scheme, or one of the many other schemes available; so there is no reason why vehicles should fail the test if maintenance policy is taken seriously. The transport manager should therefore remember that there are specific legal reasons why vehicles should be effectively maintained, besides those referred to earlier.

The need to keep informative maintenance records (i.e. inspection reports, drivers' defect reports, repair and maintenance worksheets) cannot be overemphasized; they should be kept for fifteen months from the date to which they refer.

1.4 DRIVER MANAGEMENT

The employment, training, and motivation of drivers, and the need to ensure that they work within the parameters of company procedure and the law, are also important features of transport management. The fact that drivers spend most of their time away from the depot during working hours is sufficient reason to impose driver controls where necessary. The point to bear in mind is that the effective utilization of vehicles is – to a large extent – in drivers' hands, because problems such as 'queueing' (i.e. delays due to road conditions, high-street parking restrictions, problems in finding the recipient for the goods, etc.) can only be minimized by their competence in dealing with such situations. Hence many operators employ productivity schemes to motivate drivers in improving their performance.

Productivity schemes in road transport can take a number of forms, but in most cases are geared to time saved (i.e. improvement in average speeds without breaking speed limits, and reduction of queueing time), number of drops and therefore weight or volume factors, and possibly other considerations such as type of work (whether light, heavy, or dirty), accident/incident-free record, vehicle cleanliness, and so on. Although productivity schemes vary from company to company care should always be taken to ensure that the scheme selected benefits all parties: the driver because of higher performance-related earnings; the company because of higher profitability and/or improved company image; and the customer because of a more efficient distribution service.

Motivating factors other than financial reward include: general conditions of service such as pension, sickness, and holiday schemes; social-club and sports facilities; clean vehicles and general working conditions including a uniform service; training and development opportunities; and an effective management team that inspires confidence among its employees.

The legal side of driver management must also be considered. Besides the fact that each driver must be fully qualified to drive, having regard to age and driving licences (including the H.G.V. licence where applicable), there are the matters of legal driving hours, break and rest periods, and drivers' records. Failure to comply with the regulations and orders which followed the Transport Act 1968 could involve both company *and* driver in penalty fines of up to £200 each for each offence. Employers must ensure that their drivers are issued with approved hours-of-work records for specified goods vehicles and are fully trained to use them in accordance with the prescribed regulations, and they must keep registers of the record books issued to and returned from drivers. Moreover, the records should be kept for six months (or longer if required by the licensing authority or the police) as they are open to inspection by D.o.E. inspectors and the police. Specimen records can be found in *Croner's Road Transport Operation*, a publication which is produced in loose-leaf form for revision purposes and which every transport manager should have by his side.

1.5 LOADS

Besides the vehicle and driver, special regulations are in force regarding vehicle loads. The effective transport manager should be aware of these as they cover matters such as load distribution, length and width, abnormal and dangerous loads, and various types of loads such as food, liquefied gases, radioactive materials, animals, and so on.

For example, abnormal indivisible loads and wide loads carried by a vehicle (or combination of vehicles and trailers) must not exceed the following:

Length of vehicle(s) and load: 27·4 m (metres)
Maximum width: 2·9 m (except where the load can only be safely carried on a wider vehicle or trailer which shall not exceed 6·1 m)
Maximum gross weight: 152,400 kg (kilograms)
Maximum weight on any one wheel: 11,430 kg
Speed limit: 20 miles per hour (33 km/h) where width does not exceed 2·9 m; and 12 miles per hour (20 km/h) in all other cases.

A motor vehicle and trailer carrying a load with an overall width exceeding 4·3 m but not exceeding 6·1 m is permissible *subject* to specified restrictions and conditions. The speed limit in most cases is 20 miles per hour (33 km/h).

A statutory attendant must be present: when the overall width of a vehicle or its load exceeds 3·5 m; when the overall length of a vehicle drawing a trailer or trailers and load exceeds 25·9 m; and when a vehicle carrying a load with a forward overhang exceeds 1·83 m or with a rearward projection exceeds 3·05 m.

Formal approval must be sought from the Secretary of State when a load exceeding 4·3 m in width is to be carried on the public highway. The Secretary's written notice will specify the permissible journey data such as times, dates, and route which must be adhered to.

Two clear days' notice must be given to the Chief Officer of police in each area through which a vehicle is to pass: when a vehicle exceeds 2·44 m in width and is to be driven on roads in which tramcars are used, or 2·9 m in width on other roads; when a vehicle, trailer, and load exceeds 18·3 m in length, or when a combination of vehicles, trailers, and load exceeds 25·9 m; when a forward or rearward projection of load exceeds 3·05 m; and when the gross weight exceeds 76,200 kg.

Other regulations include the issue of notices to highways and bridges authorities concerning the movement of abnormal indivisible loads in their area, the marking of projecting loads, lighting, and so on.

Regulations are also in force for special types of loads such as: food (i.e. hygiene regulations covering driver, vehicle, and facilities); dangerous loads (e.g. inflammable liquids, gases, corrosive or radioactive substances) where special regulations concerning load symbols, safety measures, notification rules, etc., apply; animals (concerning their conveyance and comfort, vehicle cleanliness, etc.); and so on.

Every transport manager should be aware of the load regulations concerning his type of business. The matters touched upon here are given full coverage in the various 'Construction and Use' and 'Authorization of Special Types' orders and regulations. While the transport manager need not be a specialist in this area he should nevertheless keep abreast of the latest legislation either by private study (perhaps using *Croner*) or by attending regular in-company up-dating sessions on all relevant aspects of road transport legislation.

1.6 INSURANCE

The matter of insurance may not necessarily be the direct responsibility of the transport manager except possibly in the case of the small company where there is no qualified officer to handle it. In other cases the transport manager will certainly be involved in fleet insurance matters if only to advise the company secretary or accountant on historic or pending changes. The wise manager will enhance his management style by learning all he can about the insurance function.

B

The first requirement of the Road Traffic Act 1972 is that all vehicles must be covered by third-party insurance. (There are certain exceptions but these will not normally affect road freight operators.) Evidence that the requirement has been met is a current certificate of insurance; without this an excise licence cannot be issued. The insurance policy must specify *inter alia*, the person or persons covered against any liability which may arise in respect of the death of or bodily injury to any person, or damage to property, caused by, or arising out of, the use of the vehicle on the road.

The requirement is basic – enough to satisfy the law – but it does no provide cover against: vehicles being damaged or stolen; the legal costs in defence of a driver who might be charged with dangerous driving; claims arising from the activities of employees other than drivers and mates (e.g. damage to property or injuries to third parties); or damage as the result of towing. Careful consideration of all the factors necessary to protect the company, followed by consultation with an authorized insurer, is therefore highly desirable. The danger of being 'uncovered' cannot be stressed too highly. At the same time, over-insurance should be avoided. Moreover, one should 'shop around' to find the best insurance rates for the cover required. An insurance company's image is also important. In most cases a comprehensive vehicle policy is necessary in view of the high cost of damage repairs which are automatically covered under this policy.

Separate cover is required for goods in transit. Operators sometimes stipulate their own conditions for the carriage of goods or adopt those laid down by the Road Haulage Association. In either case it is necessary to bring notice of the conditions to every client and indeed the insurer who arranges the cover. Where a client requires additional cover to that laid down in the conditions the operator must first obtain a written agreement from the insurer that he is willing to provide the extra cover.

Continental operations also call for sound insurance management. Besides arranging for the insurers to extend existing policies and issue an International Motor Insurance Card, the operator must also:

1 Inform his clients of the conditions of carriage relating to shipment on the Continent and beyond.
2 Ensure that subcontractors employed by him on the Continent possess the necessary insurance cover.
3 Arrange cover on the goods carried by subcontractors.

Continental operators would be wise to adopt the C.M.R. (Convention on the Contract for the International Carriage of Goods by Road) conditions of carriage, as these are recognized by most Continental countries

The operator's insurance policy should be extended as necessary to accommodate any liability which might arise under C.M.R. conditions.

Other insurance matters of interest to the effective transport manager are employer's liability insurance, which provides cover against liability for personal injury or disease sustained by employees during the course of their employment, and passenger liability insurance, which is designed to protect employees, authorized passengers, and non-fare-paying passengers who travel in company vehicles.

Workshop plant and equipment should be covered by an engineering policy.

1.7 ACTS AND REGULATIONS

The need for the transport manager to be aware of the various statutory orders and regulations which overshadow his fleet has already been stressed. This is not so difficult as it may seem, when it is remembered that every transport manager specializes in his own company's operations with familiar freight and a known fleet of vehicles. The rules and regulations applicable thereto, although possibly numerous, should not be so difficult to understand and apply in a confined company situation. A carefully structured training programme with written tests and regular up-dating would meet this important need.

The principal Acts applicable to road transport goods vehicles are:

Highways Acts 1959, 1961, and 1971
Road Traffic Acts 1960, 1962, and 1972
Road Traffic (Amendment) Act 1967
Road Traffic Regulation Act 1967
Carriage of Goods by Road Act 1968
Transport Act 1968
Vehicles and Driving Licences Act 1969
Heavy Commercial Vehicles (Controls and Regulations) Act 1973
Motor Vehicle (Constriction and Use) Regulations 1973
Goods Vehicles (Plating and Testing) Regulations 1971

1.8 OTHER TRANSPORT MATTERS

The transport manager's duties do not consist merely of those matters discussed so far. Others which concern him are those relating to fleet size, routeing and scheduling, cost control, traffic rates, workshop efficiency and expense recovery, vehicle acquisition and investment appraisal, sub-contracting or contract hire, and a host of ancillary administrative duties.

It is also his task to ensure that the company's public image is maintained at a satisfactory level through an effective delivery service.

The foregoing suggests that the transport manager should be a mature and flexible person, well organized, objective in his daily tasks, tactful in dealing with customers, his staff, and those in other departments, prepared to learn from others, willing to undergo training when necessary, and perhaps above all, prepared for change.

1.9 MANAGEMENT BY OBJECTIVES

The fact that the transport manager has to handle a multitude of duties over each working day, ranging from vehicle and driver management to miscellaneous administrative matters, stresses the need for objectivity in his job. Objectives are defined as goals or end results which a manager strives to attain. They are usually geared to a company's overall business plan which is built up from, or broken down to, branches, departments, and the managers responsible for their attainment. To be meaningful, objectives should be mutually agreed between superior and subordinate, quantified, and expressed in writing.

The value of quantified objectives is that they:

1 Provide management direction, thereby differentiating between routine administrative and management tasks.
2 Serve as management motivators in terms of financial incentives and career development.
3 Contribute to the management process and therefore to the achievement of the company's overall objectives.
4 Establish a 'management-by-objectives' – in place of a management-by-crisis – philosophy.

Even where there is no long-range business plan it is possible to have short-term goals geared to an annual operating programme, as in the case of a small haulier. The wise operator, however big or small, nevertheless plans for the future by establishing a number of meaningful objectives (*see* Chapter 17).

Objectives specific to the transport manager might include:

Vehicles

1 Fleet utilization not to be less than x per cent (or to be increased to x per cent) over the defined operating period.
2 Fleet size to be reduced by x vehicles by . . . (date).

3 A vehicle preventive-maintenance procedure to be devised in report form for the directors' consideration by . . . (date).
4 New vehicles purchased to have a payback of not less than x years.

Drivers

1 Driver turnover to be reduced to x per cent over operating year.
2 A productivity scheme to be devised for the directors' consideration by . . . (date).
3 A drivers' overall service to be introduced by . . . (date).
4 An improved driver-training scheme to increase skills of individual drivers to be developed and introduced by . . . (date).

Market

1 Company's share of the . . . (specify) market to be increased from x per cent to y per cent by . . . (date).
2 Contract with the A.B. Company for the movement of their products to be secured by . . . (date) at the rates specified in memorandum dated . . . (date).
3 A draft customer questionnaire for the consideration of the general manager to be compiled by . . . (date) in order for customer requirements to be determined and met.

Costs and profit

1 Fleet operating profit not to be less than £x over 19 . . .
2 Fixed and variable standard costs to be contained as per the agreed cost schedules.
3 The transport expenditure variance not to exceed x per cent of budget.
4 Traffic rates to be up-dated to take account of price increases by . . . (date).

Objectives should not, of course, be mere wishful statements, but rather meaningful targets agreed between the transport manager and his superior. They could be contained in the manager's annual job description or more likely in the operating budgets and schedules. The importance of appraising the manager's performance on a formal basis (say once annually) has already been mentioned. The main purpose of the appraisal is to ensure that the manager has the necessary training and resources to enable him to achieve the agreed objectives; where they are lacking they must be provided. Clearly defined objectives, resources planning, and management training are therefore closely linked and are the backbone of the successful company.
The provision of control information on a regular basis is necessary if

the transport manager is to measure his own performance (e.g. monthly cost-accounts, progress reports).

A management-by-objectives policy encourages managers to participate fully in company operations with the knowledge that the company's success is theirs also.

1.10 THE TRANSPORT MANAGER'S FUTURE ROLE

The importance attached to road freight transportation in recent years by the government, educational bodies, consultants, and academics is indicative of the rising status of the transport manager. The fact that he has *always* been important to his company, and indeed to the national economy, went unnoticed until it was realized that large cost savings could be made in the road transport sector and that the transport function is an effective part of marketing, both at home and abroad. The result is that more stringent legislation has been introduced (e.g. Transport Act 1968) to control road safety in a growing industry, and universities, colleges, and employer associations are providing courses specifically designed for the transport manager's development. The R.T.I.T.B. Motecs (Multi-Occupational Training and Education Centres) run a number of courses throughout the year on costing and accounting, transport management, international operations, etc., which are always heavily subscribed by both in-scope (haulage) and out-of-scope (own-account) managers. Qualifications are obtainable with any of the professional transport bodies, including the Chartered Institute of Transport, although qualifications are nothing new. New diploma and degree courses in transport and physical distribution have been introduced over the last few years, and graduates in transport management are now increasing their number.

There is every indication that the transport manager will therefore become more and more professional, principally because of the ever-increasing demands being made upon him and the educational and training environment suddenly surrounding him.

While the transport manager's necessary qualities (such as those outlined in section 1.8) will not change, his approach to the transport function will nevertheless be quite different from that of the past. He will most certainly use mathematical models and employ computer services for determining the optimum fleet size, and routeing and scheduling operations; while fleet management in general involving control ratios, break-even analysis, discounted cash flow, and other related management techniques will no doubt form part of his everyday work routine.

1.11 SUMMARY

1 The use of management job descriptions is important in that they give a clear guide as to the purpose of each job function, define responsibilities and relationships, and list the resources which the manager has available to achieve the objectives of his job.

2 Customer marketing research is essential if customers' changing needs are to be met. The use of a questionnaire or direct discussion with each customer to determine his requirements would assist the transport operator in gearing his business for change.

3 Vehicle mangement includes their effective maintenance, their replacement and the observation of current legislation concerning vehicle safety.

4 The management of drivers includes their employment, training, and motivation, and the adherence to current legislation concerning driving hours, break and rest periods, and the maintenance of drivers' records in prescribed form.

5 Besides vehicle and driver legislation the transport manager should be aware of the legislation covering loads, as regards weight, dimensions, and type of load.

6 The transport manager should ensure that his vehicles, drivers, passengers, goods in transit, equipment, etc., are adequately covered against liability or loss by an authorized insurer. The company's conditions of carriage, both in the United Kingdom and on the Continent, should be brought to customers' notice (e.g. on the back of company stationery). Any requirements over and above the conditions should first be cleared with the authorized insurer before acceptance of the customer's order.

7 In-company training programmes with written tests at regular intervals are a good way of ensuring that the transport manager keeps abreast of the various Acts and regulations applicable to his type of business.

8 Management by objectives provides clearly defined directives as to what has to be done, when, where, how, and by whom, and thus motivates managers to participate fully in company operations and so achieve the company's overall objectives.

9 The transport manager's future role is seen to be a more professional one in view of the interest recently shown in his development by universities, colleges, transport bodies, and other organizations. Already graduates in transport management are increasing their number.

A / 658.91

2 Fleet Size

2.1 THE PROBLEM OF FLEET SIZE

Many transport operators carry out their daily task of delivering goods to various points up and down the country, and if perchance some of their vehicles are idle for part of the time it is put down to lack of orders or poor utilization. Little do they realize that they should gear capacity to demand, rather than maintain a fleet of vehicles just because they have always had vehicles of that quantity, weight, and class. Consequently it is easy to have too many vehicles employed. A smaller fleet of the 'right size' could earn a higher return on the capital employed. The problem lies in determining the fleet size requirement.

2.2 FACTORS AFFECTING FLEET SIZE

These will depend upon a number of interrelated factors, namely:

1 Anticipated total traffic demand.
2 Whether special- or general-purpose traffic.
3 Seasonal fluctuations in demand.
4 Number of depots and customer location points.
5 Level of subcontract work (hauliers), use of carriers (own-account), or vehicle hire.
6 Design and capacity.
7 Routeing, loading, and scheduling techniques.
8 Operating efficiency.
9 Driver availability.
10 Return on capital.

Items 9 and 10 may appear superfluous at first sight, but unless there is an adequate supply of trained drivers to man the planned fleet of vehicles, and unless the anticipated return on investment is worthwhile, there is little point in investing in further vehicles when the use of carriers might provide a better solution.

No hard and fast rules can be laid down as fleet size must remain an individual company problem. Generally speaking the haulier requires the maximum return on the minimum fleet investment, while the own-account operator's aim is the maximum utilization of vehicles at minimum cost in meeting the company's transport requirements. In either case fleet size is the criterion.

2.3 CONFLICTING FACTORS

If a fleet is undersize an operator must weigh up the cost of hiring, sub-contracting, or employing carriers – depending on whether it is a haulage or own-account operation – against the cost of purchasing. This should present no problem as a cost comparison table can easily be compiled (*see*, for example, Chapter 14) and a decision made accordingly. There would be little point in acquiring another vehicle to solve an immediate transport problem if the vehicle is to stand idle in the yard for most of the year. Subcontracting or the employment of carriers would solve the problem providing the action was cost-effective.

The decision to *increase* fleet size is usually a straightforward one and is based on the return expected from the investment: profit in the case of a haulier, and cost savings in the case of an own-account operator, although they amount to the same thing.

What if a fleet is oversize? This may be difficult to determine unless vehicles are standing around idle. Most fleets are busy on the road some-where whether they are being usefully employed or not; the expression 'keeping the wheels turning' may be interpreted too literally at the expense of efficiency. Such a situation can only be detected by reappraising the trans-port scheduling system. This would involve examination of the factors outlined above, namely, the anticipated total load, broken down to areas, types of traffic and therefore types and sizes of vehicles, routes and times involved, and so on. Allowances would have to be made for 'off-road' time and possibly spare vehicles to take account of contingencies. The appraisal is by no means easy and requires very careful analysis if the result is to be meaningful.

Some of the size factors may conflict with others, for example: where the overall fleet size does not mean an even utilization throughout the year because of seasonal variations in trade; where there is a severe shortage of drivers to man the requisite number of vehicles; and where additional vehicles are required but the competitive rates or operating costs do not make it a viable proposition. In all these cases it is a matter of deciding what is best for the company or department in the medium to long term. A short-term solution might be to subcontract or use carriers, even though operating costs would very likely rise. A longer-term solution would be to increase the fleet investment, obtain and train an adequate driver force (perhaps by offering more competitive pay and conditions), and utilize the fleet to the full by attracting additional traffic.

2.4 VEHICLE DESIGN AND CAPACITY

It is no use talking about numbers without prior consideration of the *types* of vehicles required. Vehicle types and their number will depend upon the nature and volume of the traffic to be carried. The following types of vehicles might be used for the purpose stated:

1 *Platform:* (*a*) general purpose, where the load is covered by a tarpaulin; or (*b*) with sides where 'loose' loads (e.g. gravel) are carried, often fitted with tipping gear.
2 *Box:* where loads need covered protection (e.g. parcels and removals).
3 *Articulated:* (*a*) where loading and unloading time is a crucial factor – the tractor and driver are thus released for other work; or (*b*) where temporary storage is required.
4 *Specials:* e.g. tankers (e.g. milk, fuel), concrete mixers, tippers.

The number of each type depends upon the nature and volume of traffic, distances, and drops to be made. Clearly the longer a round trip and the larger the number of drops, then the larger the vehicle required, all things being equal. But if deliveries are spasmodic then possibly a medium-size vehicle would suffice.

Vehicle design and use should therefore be geared to the job function to ensure maximum suitability of vehicle and load.

2.5 TRAILERS

Mention is made in Chapters 7 and 10 of the ratio of trailers to tractors which ensures that the company's operations are adequately covered.

Besides the tractor–trailer operating ratio there is the matter of the trailers which are hired out to other operators for reward. As this activity affects fleet size the operator must ensure that his trailers are fully utilized and that the return on their investment is adequate. Bearing in mind that current interest rates are the highest in years, an operator must ask himself whether the outlay in trailers, their upkeep, and the income arising from them produce more than the average rate of return after tax. It is true that trailers may appreciate in value if carefully maintained and this should be taken into account. There is little point, however, in providing a trailer service for other operators at the expense of one's own operations. Operators should therefore examine this activity very carefully.

2.6 CONTRACTING OUT

By extending the same reasoning to a complete vehicle or fleet service, the belief may be held that the more vehicles hired out the higher the reward. This may be true in one sense, but an efficient hire company will seek to have the minimum number of vehicles per customer as possible. The reasoning here is twofold:

1 There would be more vehicles available to serve other hirers.
2 Cost-effectiveness is enhanced within the hiring company, thus establishing an excellent relationship between contractor and hirer.

One of the largest contract hire companies in the United Kingdom has a contract with an association of fish merchants on the east coast. The contract is serviced by a number of trunk- and local-delivery vehicles. Although the association has increased its output the number of vehicles employed has actually been reduced as the result of more effective working methods, thereby enhancing cost-effectiveness. Thus both parties gain: the company because of an enhanced reputation and increased trade; and the hirer through a more efficient distribution service at realistic cost.

Care should therefore be taken in the acquisition of 'contract' vehicles, which should be tailor-made to customer requirements.

2.7 GEOGRAPHICAL CONSIDERATIONS

Apart from the problems of routeing (discussed later), the geographical spread of transport activities will also affect the fleet size. Areas of dense population and sparsely populated areas may each require different treatment. In the first case it is possible to have a number of distribution points, each serviced by its own fleet of local-delivery vehicles. In the second case it may be necessary to have one central base where bulk consignments for each user can be broken down and consolidated into delivery rounds.

A well-known national carrier follows this second procedure by having, for example, a central distribution centre in Glasgow to serve the Lowlands and Highlands. Full loads are trunked at night from the production unit in central England to the distribution centre. Orders for Lowland destinations are then delivered within forty-eight hours of despatch from the production unit, and for Highland destinations within five days. Vehicles to cover the operation are organized accordingly. An exclusive service such as this is preferable to the manufacturer having his own local-delivery arrangements, which could be extremely costly.

2.8 OPERATING EFFICIENCY

Fleet operating efficiency is a crucial factor in fleet size. To the uninitiated, road transport is a relatively simple activity when compared with, say, manufacturing, and is a matter of carrying goods from A to B. In the case of the small haulier/distributor this may be so, but for the vast majority of operators there are a large number of variables to consider, which call for a high degree of planning if operating efficiency is to be attained. Among these variables may be numerous collection/delivery points up and down the country, fluctuating customer demands, different volumes and types of traffic, special-order requirements, varying road conditions, speed and vehicle restrictions, and so on, all of which have to be met from an existing fleet of vehicles of different types and capacities. Moreover, the vehicles have to be effectively maintained and to meet stringent legal requirements if they are to stay on the road. Then there are other factors such as driver availability, training and absenteeism, weather conditions, accidents, and the like. The organized operator should consolidate the many variables and aim to utilize his fleet in the most effective manner, meeting customer demand at the lowest possible cost. An efficient operator would therefore require less vehicles than an inefficient operator in charge of the same operation.

The part that drivers have to play is very important. Many of them know areas, routes, and locations better than anyone else, and they frequently have to put their knowledge into practice when confronted with problems such as flooding, subsidence, road accidents, etc. Possibly more miles are saved through their competence than through any routeing system devised in the traffic office. Very often their advice is required before routeing systems are established.

Although it is important to save operating miles it is more important to save the real costs of road transportation: namely, vehicle fixed and investment costs.

2.9 REDUCING 'EXTERNAL' TRANSPORT COSTS

A common feature of road freight operations is the need to hire vehicles, subcontract work, use carrier services, or employ specialist contract services from time to time. Since it usually costs more to 'use' other operators' vehicles because of the profit element, operators should attempt to reduce the employment of other operators' services. This may not be entirely possible, however, for a number of reasons (e.g. supply and demand factors, investment problems, seasonal fluctuations, company agreements) and contract service is probably a special case anyway. Journey planning should nevertheless be logistically planned so that external services are used as little as possible. It might be found, for example, that company-owned vehicles can be used for all long-distance work and also for town work where the traffic volume is high, leaving the residual – perhaps unimportant – traffic to be dealt with by other operators.

Careful analysis and planning are necessary if external transport costs are to be minimized. For this reason the entire routeing and scheduling system should be reappraised, starting with company-owned vehicles and the more important customer/distribution services, working down to the not-so-important services. Once company vehicle capacity/operating time is used up attention can then be paid to external transport services. A number of cost models may be necessary to find the best transport solution.

Hired vehicles, etc., are therefore very much a part of fleet size planning and cannot be ignored.

2.10 VEHICLE LOADING

Another factor frequently ignored by operators which has a profound effect on fleet size is that of vehicle loading. Sometimes referred to as the 'knapsack problem' it is primarily concerned with the *physical* loading of a commodity into a confined space. In this context it should not be confused with vehicle scheduling (the term 'loading' being used sometimes instead of 'scheduling').

The expression that you cannot get more than a pint into a pint pot is relevant here; but it is very easy to get less than a pint in, which can easily happen when loading goods vehicles. The carriage of spare capacity per vehicle per day over the total number of fleet operating days per annum can be an expensive business, and to some extent makes nonsense of route planning.

The loading problem is less acute where specialized equipment is used (e.g. pallets, tankers, containers) because it can be seen at a glance where spare capacity exists. But freight such as parcels (which are often anything but brown-paper packages, e.g. motorcycles, ladders, barrels, plants, crates), household removals, and manufactured goods of various shapes and sizes, requires special attention. 'Two-stage loading', which involves loading or packing boxes into larger boxes and then accommodating the larger boxes, is not uncommon, but has its problems. For example, the dimensions of palletized units and vehicle 'boxes' must be compatible if capacity is to be fully utilized.

The loading problem is therefore concerned with minimizing the number of vehicles required for a given array of consignments (i.e. volume and weight) and frequencies (trips and drops) by effective physical loading. Although operators absorb the problem as part of the scheduling procedure the importance of its effect upon fleet size should not be forgotten.

2.11 SUMMARY

1 The object of fleet size appraisal is to minimize the number of vehicles required for a given volume of traffic, trips, and drops, thus saving the real costs of road transportation, namely, investment and vehicle fixed costs.

2 Fleet size should not be taken for granted but should be reviewed regularly as part of strategic planning.

3 A number of factors can affect fleet size, the precise mix of which can vary from company to company. Therefore no hard and fast rules can be laid down and each company should establish its own key factors in order to determine the most favourable fleet size.

4 Vehicles should be chosen which ensure maximum suitability to freight requirements in terms of design and capacity.

5 Contract hire vehicles (including trailers), which form part of fleet size, should be fully utilized (except for 'spares' kept for emergencies) if they are to earn their keep.

6 The use of external transport services should be restricted to the less-important customer/distribution services, involving where possible the least period of time.

7 Physical loading is very much a part of the fleet size problem. Spare capacity per vehicle per day over the total number of fleet operating days is a loss contributor. The aim of effective loading is to utilize capacity to the full and save vehicles.

3 Vehicle Routeing and Depot Siting

3.1 THE ROUTEING PROBLEM

3.1.1 PURPOSE OF VEHICLE ROUTEING

Routeing is defined as the maximum utilization of vehicles at minimum cost. In fact there is more to it than that. Minimum cost is often identified as operating cost, i.e. variable cost savings through better routeing, which loses sight of vehicle fixed costs and investment costs which could be saved if fewer vehicles were employed for the same volume of traffic. Simply keeping the wheels turning at the maximum does not necessarily mean effective vehicle utilization. The aim should therefore be the *maximum employment of the minimum number of vehicles over the shortest possible distances*. This would ensure a highly effective transport system at minimum operating costs and minimum investment.

3.1.2 FACTORS AFFECTING ROUTEING

These are:
1 Fleet size.
2 Design and capacity.
3 Number of collection/delivery points.
4 Number and location of depots.
5 Driver and vehicle restraints (e.g. driving laws, maintenance requirements).
6 Time, distances, and speeds.
7 Population density (e.g. in busy cities and difficult areas such as the Highlands and the West Country).
8 Road conditions (e.g. 'B' roads, motorways).
9 Type of traffic (e.g. livestock, perishables).
10 Special distribution requirements.
11 Number of drops.
12 Call time.

While most of these factors are common to all operators there will no doubt be others which are peculiar to the individual operator. Again the starting point would be the type and volume of traffic and the required fleet mix and size. But economies in the precise number of vehicles will not be possible until close attention has been paid to routeing.

3.1.3 ROUTEING IS NOT EASY

Any problem involving a large number of variables is not easy. In fact, the higher the number the stronger the case for employing computer services, but even then the pattern of variables may change overnight and necessitate further programming. Where deliveries are fairly regular to specific points over selected routes where consumption is fairly constant (e.g. possibly bread supplies to outlets), there is no real problem. But such situations are few and far between, and most operators have problems of one sort or another. In fact, most routeing systems leave much to be desired because, more often than not, it is a scientific problem in the hands of unscientific men.

A number of methods have been developed to resolve the problems of route planning. Some of them are referred to in section 3.4 where it will be seen that the suggested solutions can be no more than a general guide. It is therefore up to each operator to take his own routeing problem seriously. The result is likely to be a 'good' routeing system rather than the ideal one.

3.2 THE DEPOT PROBLEM

Depot (or warehouse) siting precedes route planning for obvious reasons. Essentially it is a costing problem because it involves the cost of transporting goods in bulk to the depot, depot operating costs, and the cost of delivering goods to customers. The smaller the number of depots the greater the local transportation costs. Conversely, the more depots there are the higher the investment costs but the lower the local fleet operating costs. But as the latter would clash with higher depot operating and bulk transport costs there may not be any advantage whatsoever. A number of cost models are therefore necessary to find the optimal solution involving the lowest operating costs.

The real problem lies in deciding how many depots there should be and their precise location. The majority of transport companies are already 'stuck' with their depots, but even so it is possible to reorganize their number and location if it is advantageous – long-term – to do so. Besides the divestment and reinvestment problem, consideration should also be given to the effect on depot personnel – their mobility, possible redundancy, replacement, and training. Other considerations are: location, throughput, size, operating costs, delivery radius, and whether to rent or buy.

Sufficient has been said so far to show that fleet size, depot siting (including their number), and vehicle routeing are all closely interrelated, and that consideration of any of these in isolation is highly impracticable.

3.3 METHODS OF DEPOT SITING

Methods vary from the scientific to the heuristic. The majority of operators prefer the heuristic approach (i.e. by logical reasoning rather than scientific analysis which perhaps involves complex mathematics) because they claim that it reduces the problem to a manageable size which is understood by all. Even so, no manager should turn a blind eye to new methods without first giving them a try.

Much has been written on depot siting during the last decade, both in the United Kingdom and abroad; but the problem of the number, location, size, and customer allocation remains very much a personal company problem. In the final analysis the best location(s) is the one(s) that provides the best customer service for the least cost.

3.3.1 THE KEEFER METHOD FOR LOCATING A SINGLE DEPOT

This involves the employment of a piece of plywood which has been cut out in the shape of the area to be served. A small hole is drilled at each customer location point and a weight, suspended on a string, hangs down from each hole, the weights varying according to the volume of customer demand over the year. The point where the model can be evenly balanced is reckoned to be the ideal depot location point. The technique is sometimes called the 'centre of gravity' method.

The fact that this method was introduced many years ago suggests that it should be regarded with caution. For one thing, single-depot siting is really a 'one-off' problem; and while taking account of throughput, etc., at the time of making the decision the technique does not allow for changing patterns in demand. Neither does it overcome the problem of the terrain (mountains, rivers, etc.) or the unavailability of or impossibility of finding a suitable site in the selected area. Since its introduction the method has been further developed by others, but such problems remain a stumbling block.

3.3.2 THE GEOGRAPHIC-DEMAND METHOD FOR LOCATING A SINGLE DEPOT

Where there are a number of 'demand locations' involving a number of customer clusters, a depot should be sited in or nearest to the location with the biggest demand.

If there were two demand locations, A and B, and A had the largest demand, the depot should be sited at A, leaving the smaller volume of goods to be delivered to B, thus reducing transport costs. If A and B had similar demands then the depot could be sited at A *or* B *or* between the two. If there were three demand locations, A, B, and C, the depot should be sited at the location with the largest demand in relation to the combined demand of the other two: for example, at B if the demand factors were A_1, B_3, C_1.

The same reasoning can be applied to any number of demand locations, but the wider they are apart and the closer the demand factors, then the more difficult the siting problem.

3.3.3 THE GEOGRAPHIC-DEMAND METHOD FOR LOCATING A NUMBER OF DEPOTS

Several approaches are available, but the most popular is dividing the country into areas or regions (the precise number depending upon the scale of operations) and then pinpointing the demand in each area. The latter may be based on historical data (e.g. annual sales) or market forecasts, whichever is preferred by the operator. The wise operator would take past data into account and adjust it according to known or expected changes.

In a multi-depot system it may be necessary to divide the country into control regions and then into operating areas (possibly then into sub-areas) if depot siting is to be logical. Consideration would also be given to vehicle *size* before reaching a decision, as this could affect the number of delivery points which form delivery groups (i.e. the larger the vehicle then presumably the higher the number of drops per journey). Although this is predominantly a routeing problem it should nevertheless be borne in mind at this critical stage.

The projected throughput for each region or area should be sufficient to determine the possible number of depots required. Their precise location should preferably be towards the centre of the demand area and have regard to:

1 The availability of a suitable site which has the necessary services including planning permission for extensions.
2 The availability of suitable labour.
3 Access to road and rail networks, sea and air terminals, as required by the business.
4 Projected throughput.
5 Peculiar or special customer requirements.
6 The cost of trunking, depot and local transport costs.

7 The employment of contract services.
8 Investment considerations: whether to buy or rent, return on investment, etc.

A number of possible sitings in a particular area might be chosen – say two or three – and a priority list drawn up. Item 6 – costing – requires detailed analysis, especially the local transport side, which takes us back to the routeing problem. Briefly, selected routeings would be based on the number of delivery points, the number of drops, delivery times, and so on. The closer the depot to those points with the heaviest demand the higher the cost savings.

3.3.4 ALTERNATIVES TO AREA DEPOTS

It is possible to have, say, two or three depots per *region*, rather than area, to serve all the areas within it, particularly in regions such as the South-West or the Lowlands and Highlands, depending of course on the type and rate of demand. On the other hand it might be preferable to employ contract services and so save the investment in depots. The advantages of specialist contract hire services can be very appealing, as for example:

1 The employment of other operators' resources including maintenance and extra vehicles as and when required.
2 The employment of fleet management services (e.g. drivers, insurance, licensing, testing, garaging, cleaning).
3 The saving of capital outlay.
4 A predetermined hire charge which is an allowable tax expense.
5 An accurate basis for budgeting and expenditure control.

These points equally apply to hauliers who may wish to employ vehicles under a contract hire agreement.

An alternative, which could be applied in certain circumstances only (e.g. where depots are few in number), would be to deliver to customers direct from the factory and so dispense with depots altogether, if the various circumstances allow.

3.4 METHODS OF VEHICLE ROUTEING

A method of vehicle routeing must aim to marry a number of variables such as distance, speeds, number of drops, call times, etc., with a fleet of vehicles employed from specific locations (depots) in order to meet the varying demands of customers in the most effective way.

Routeing methods can be either manual – which are by far the most common – or computerized. Both types start with the basic principle of using map grid references in relation to customer locations. The separate (or sometimes conjoined) references thus become the groups in which customer demand is determined. The 'demand' can be expressed in so many units per period of time, matched with vehicle capacities, and a suitable route can then be calculated to ensure that the deliveries can be made within the allotted time. It is the latter which causes most of the problems.

Ways of solving the problem were tackled some years ago by a number of thinkers who among them developed the 'travelling-salesmen' and 'distance-savings' methods.

3.4.1 TRAVELLING-SALESMEN METHOD

This method was developed in the 1930s in order to save salesmen's time and the distance from their starting point to their farthest point and back again. Applied to transport the object was to save vehicle miles and thereby reduce operating costs (i.e. fuel, oil, tyres, etc.). Naturally the idea applied in particular to those operators who ran trips from a fixed point to known destinations with specified loads and back again, thus leaving the general haulier out in the cold. It did not take long to realize, however, that scientific routeing could be applied to most transport operations and that the ultimate aim was to save vehicles besides mileage.

3.4.2 DISTANCE-SAVINGS METHOD

The savings method was developed on the assumption that miles need to be minimized when vehicle capacity is limited. It consists of joining a number of delivery points on a map into pairs in order to select the best routes. Thus the nearest two delivery points are paired, then the next nearest pair, and so on, until the optimum route is established which satisfies customer requirements in the necessary time span. The method is nevertheless a difficult one to apply in practice where, for example, there are numerous clusters of delivery points in a demand area. A way around the problem is to assume that each customer is a single call in a round trip and then to link in other calls to reduce trips to and from the depot.

3.4.3 PIN-AND-STRING METHOD

Yet another method involves the use of pins and string. A model representing the area under consideration is constructed (e.g. a piece of plywood cut to shape, or simply a square or oblong with the boundaries clearly marked). Pins representing each customer location are driven into the model. A piece of string is then cut to length for each type of vehicle, the length representing the vehicle's daily availability in terms of distance and capacity. Routes are then selected by trial and error, by starting each string from the depot and passing it around a number of pins. Queueing problems at customer points are dealt with by winding the string around the relevant pins a number of times according to the average delay. Spare string – i.e. loose ends – represents spare time and capacity. Steps are taken to rectify this by re-routeing until full capacity is utilized.

The pin-and-string method may be suitable in certain cases (e.g. where delivery locations are widely dispersed, such as in trunking), but where customer clusters are dense, such as in a large city, the method is cumbersome.

3.4.4 PIGEON HOLE SYSTEM

A fairly common manual method of routeing, used by both own-account and haulage operators, is the pigeon hole system. The system is designed to cover a particular region, area, or zone, and usually resembles the map pattern of the area in terms of boundaries and contained locations. For example, the pigeon hole for the Medway towns (Chatham, Gillingham, Rochester, and Strood) would be north of the Hastings, Bexhill, and Eastbourne pigeon hole, thus facilitating the scheduling process. The scheduler allocates orders to the various pigeon holes; these are then scheduled into the vehicle loads per customer, delivery times, etc. which make up the journey sheet. If there is spare vehicle capacity it may be necessary to incorporate other journeys or to delay the trip – i.e. hold over – until capacity can be filled, if circumstances will allow and the vehicles can be fully utilized on other trips.

Another method is to sort orders into geographic customer loads and delivery times – perhaps dealing with priority customers first – and produce a delivery schedule, working from a map in order to save delivery trip time. The loads are then allocated to the most suitable vehicles or those which are available.

In both methods daily or weekly trips are arranged as necessary.

3.5 COMPUTER SERVICES

Brief mention has been made earlier of the employment of computer services where a problem involves a large number of variables. Routeing variables are by no means limited in number and therefore readily lend themselves to computer programming.

Many operators are still suspicious of computer systems and prefer to rely on their own experienced schedulers who, it is claimed, know their areas, customers, vehicles, drivers, routes, and problems far better than a piece of electronic hardware. It is true that a computer is not endowed with a 'thinking' or 'judgement' faculty. Its sole function is to add, subtract, multiply, and divide; but it has a vast appetite for absorbing volume and producing a host of pertinent information that is essential for decision making and control. Moreover, its employment in routeing problems has already proved successful in a number of cases in saving both vehicles and miles.

Savings made from the use of a computer do not happen overnight, however. First the computer must be taught to behave like an experienced scheduler; it should, for example, be able to read maps, relate orders to locations, compile delivery groups, allocate loads to vehicles, and so on. Once the computer has been taught to do everything that an experienced scheduler can do, it is a matter of improving upon his performance. At this juncture two points should be borne in mind: the first is that the improvement in cost savings should at least cover the cost of the computer system; the second is that when circumstances change (e.g. through flooding, road repairs, driver absenteeism, mechanical breakdown, last-minute orders) re-programming will be necessary. In this last respect manual routeing is often (but not always) more flexible than the computer system.

Trip-planning 'programs' have been devised by a number of computer firms and in many cases can be tailor-made to suit the particular requirements of an operator. Current programs include a variety of trade names such as VANTRAN (International Computers Ltd), VANSCHED (National Cash Register Co. Ltd), and so on. Information is available from any of the national computer firms or through the National Computing Centre in Manchester. The latter body has conducted a survey among companies engaged in transport and distribution, regarding scheduling problems. Its findings and the part that computers have to play in problem solving are given in its publication *Computers in Vehicle Scheduling* which makes interesting reading.

3.6 SUMMARY

1 The object of routeing is to save miles, time, and sometimes vehicles.
2 Routeing is not always easy because it usually involves a large number of variables. Regular delivery services facilitate good routeing, but irregular services require special routeing attention.

3 The number and location of depots have an important bearing on route planning. Depots should preferably be located in or near high-demand areas to reduce local delivery costs. Their precise number and investment and trunking costs should be considered very carefully as part of strategic planning.

4 A number of routeing methods are available ranging from the use of pins and string to advanced computer route-planning systems.

5 Trip-planning 'programs' have been devised by a number of computer firms and can be tailor-made to meet the particular requirements of a distributor.

Part Two

COSTING AND PRICING
FLEET OPERATIONS

4 Why Costing is Necessary

4.1 LIMITATIONS OF FINANCIAL ACCOUNTS

The annual financial accounts of a business are by themselves of little use for control purposes. For one thing they are produced far too late after a financial year has ended to be of any real service; for another, they are produced in such form as to make the extraction of pertinent control information difficult if not impossible. If quarterly or monthly accounts were promptly produced management would at least know how much a business was making or losing overall, but it would not know where profits were being made or where losses were being incurred. The following simple illustration should make this clear.

A. Haulier Ltd operates a mixed fleet of six vehicles which carry a variety of traffic ranging from livestock to wide loads. The accounts for the last trading year show the following results:

Turnover	£100,000
less Costs and overheads	(£90,000)
Profit before taxation	£10,000

The accounts show that the business has made a return of 10 per cent on turnover before taxation, which might be considered satisfactory. But where a cost-accounting system is employed – i.e. where revenue, costs, and expenses are systematically analysed over vehicles – the cost accounts might show the following true position:

Vehicle	Revenue	Costs and overheads	Profit/(Loss)
	£	£	£
1	13,000	14,000	(1,000)
2	27,000	29,000	(2,000)
3	18,000	13,000	5,000
4	12,000	8,000	4,000
5	16,000	16,000	—
6	14,000	10,000	4,000
	100,000	90,000	10,000

Assuming that costs have been properly allocated and overheads equitably apportioned, the position now is not so good; there are losses in the case of two vehicles and no profit at all in the case of a third. These points are completely hidden in the annual accounts, as is the fact that the vehicle with the highest turnover is the one with the biggest loss. Quite clearly a more dynamic form of reporting is required which would highlight adverse trends as they occurred rather than after the event, when it is too late to take corrective action.

Costing does just that.

4.2 THE IMPORTANCE OF COSTING

While in recent years most industries have been affected in one way or another by rising prices and burdensome legislation, the problem has been particularly acute in the road transport industry. As a result many small firms have gone out of business, being unable to withstand the double effect of inflation and restriction.

It is a fact of life, however, that where a cost-accounting system is employed, *and* used, a business has a much better chance of survival. This is because unfavourable trends are at once brought to light so that management can take corrective action. Put another way, costing by itself solves nothing, but it does present management with facts and relevant information which enable them to make more accurate decisions. In short, it helps them to manage a business more effectively by not leaving the most important side of the business – the financial side – to run its own course.

The re-analysed accounts of A. Haulier Ltd show quite clearly that the company lost £2,000 on the biggest part of its turnover (27 per cent, vehicle 2) and that 56 per cent of the work undertaken during the year was completely useless (vehicles 1, 2, and 5). Had the company employed a costing system the unhealthy trend would have shown itself quite early in the year, so that management could have acted: first, by ascertaining the reasons for the loss (e.g. inaccurate estimating, poor maintenance, bad utilization, high overheads); and secondly, by taking whatever steps were necessary to correct the situation.

4.3 THE COST OF COSTING

A costing system entails the use of forms and human effort. In an industry where costing is so scant it means having to employ suitable staff, which many hauliers claim they cannot afford to do. The irony is that a vast number of hauliers are already losing lots of money but do not know it, because there is no reporting system to bring losses to their attention! True, they receive the historical annual accounts which tell them how much they have made or lost over the trading year – and very often this comes as a shock – but too frequently the annual accounts contain hidden losses, as we saw from the re-analysed accounts of A. Haulier Ltd.

The fact is that no business can be properly – and profitably – run without some form of financial reporting. The cost of financing that reporting should be regarded as an investment that will enhance the profitability of the business.

If, for example, A. Haulier Ltd had employed an experienced costing clerk for £1,000 per annum and, as a result of the information produced, had managed to eliminate the losses in the case of vehicles 1 and 2, the net addition to profit before taxation would have been £2,000:

	£
Profit (vehicles 3–6)	13,000
less Additional salary	(1,000)
	12,000
less Original profit	(10,000)
Additional profit	2,000

4.4 COSTING AND ESTIMATING

Costing and estimating are often regarded as one and the same thing. In fact they are quite different, although estimating is often assisted by basic costing information. Costing, in the historical sense, is nothing more than the recording of actual costs after they have been incurred. Estimating, on the other hand, is concerned with rate fixing, i.e. fixing a price for some future job or contract.

We would like to think that traffic rates were based on known costs plus an uplift for profit. But in an industry where costing is just beginning to emerge it is apparent that this assumption cannot possibly be so, and that it could well be one of the reasons why the return on capital in road haulage is low compared with that in other industries. In practice, traffic rates are based on factors besides those of cost. These are dealt with later where it is shown that estimating has a very important part to play in the success of a transport business.

Suffice it to say that the revenue figures shown in the accounts of A. Haulier Ltd are the result of accepted estimates or rates, while the costs shown in the same accounts are the actual costs incurred.

4.5 THE MEANING OF COSTING

The term 'costing' as used here is really an abbreviation of the more descriptive name 'cost accounting'. Put very simply, cost accounting traces costs to causes and is primarily concerned with the effective use of resources

– materials, men, machines, and money. This concept should never be lost sight of because that is what costing is all about. Costing records, traces, and measures. In a road haulage firm (or transport department) costs and profits are analysed over vehicles (or groups of vehicles), depots, and internal departments. It shows 'at a glance' where profits and losses are being made and where management action is needed most.

A business without a costing system has been likened to a ship without a compass and a lighthouse without a lamp.

4.6 WHY COSTING IS NECESSARY

Costing is therefore necessary in road transport operations for these reasons:

1 To give regular up-to-date information on profitability: for the business as a whole, for depots, for individual-vehicle operations, and for different types of traffic.
2 To highlight adverse trends so that management can take the appropriate corrective action.
3 To enable management to determine the extent to which rates may be allowed to fall during severe competition.
4 To assist rate fixing by the inclusion of basic costing data.
5 To increase the return on capital employed.

4.7 KEY TO PROFITABILITY

Enough has been said to show that costing is an important key to profitability. To be effective, however, the key must be in the right hands. Management must be able to interpret costing data as it is produced and take suitable corrective action where things go wrong and profits fall. Costing should therefore be a continuous systematic process rather than a slipshod affair resulting in untidy figures on the back of an envelope, for costing provides the basis for decision making and control.

4.8 SUMMARY

1 Financial accounts are not sufficiently detailed to show management where profits and losses are being made. A costing system provides this information and also enhances cost reduction and control.
2 The cost of costing should be regarded as an investment rather than an expense, because a proper costing system enhances profitability.
3 Although costing and estimating are allied they are not quite the same:

costing is the recording of actual costs as they are incurred; estimating is concerned with price fixing for the future.

4 Costing is primarily concerned with the effective use of resources – labour, materials, vehicles, equipment, and money.

5 Costing provides pertinent control information vital to company profitability and growth.

5 Introduction to Costing and Road Transport Costs

No treatise on costing should be attempted without first giving an appreciation of basic costing terminology so far as it applies to the industry under discussion.

5.1 COSTING TERMINOLOGY

5.1.1 COST UNIT

A 'cost unit' is a unit of quantity in which costs may be ascertained or expressed. The classic example in road transport is, of course, the 'kilometre run' or even the 'tonne-kilometre'. Other units are the tonne, cubic metre, litre, load, pack, etc., depending on the type of traffic carried and the particular unit of measurement required.

5.1.2 COST CENTRE

A 'cost centre' – or *control* centre – is a location, person, or piece of equipment against which costs are charged. A typical example is a vehicle which is charged with annual costs (licence, insurance, depreciation, etc.) and operating costs (wages, fuel, maintenance, etc.). Another example is a workshop which is charged with rent, rates, electricity, wages, depreciation, insurance, and so on.

In a transport business with a large fleet of vehicles a *group* of vehicles of a particular weight and class (e.g. artics, tippers, tankers) could be considered together and called a cost centre.

A combined example of a cost unit and cost centre can be seen in a workshop. All relevant costs are charged to the workshop cost centre; they are then recovered from the vehicles which pass through that cost centre, the vehicles in this case being the cost units.

5.1.3 DIRECT COSTS

A direct cost is a cost which is directly identifiable and therefore directly chargeable to a cost centre or cost unit. Driver's wages, fuel, oil, tyres, licence, insurance, repairs, etc. are all direct costs which are directly chargeable to a vehicle cost centre. Similarly, fitters' wages and space costs are direct costs in the case of a workshop cost centre and are recoverable from the vehicles served (i.e. the cost units).

5.1.4 INDIRECT COSTS

These are costs which are not wholly identifiable with a cost centre or cost unit but which can be apportioned to cost centres and cost units. Management and administrative expenses, for example, cannot be charged to any particular vehicle or workshop activity but can be apportioned over an entire fleet of vehicles using some suitable basis.

5.1.5 FIXED COSTS

A fixed cost is a cost which does not vary with 'mileage' or vehicle activity. As most fixed costs are fixed in the short term only – due to inflation and change of circumstance – it can be argued that no cost is ever really fixed. From the costing point of view, however, these costs are fixed in the sense that they exist whether vehicles operate or not. For example, if an operator's fleet of vehicles suddenly seized up on the road he would, initially, be non-operational; even so he would still have to pay his fixed costs (salaries, rent, rates, telephone charges, etc.). A better example is that of a vehicle. Before a vehicle is allowed to operate on the highway the transport operator must first incur certain annual or fixed costs – road licence, insurance, depreciation, etc. These costs must be met whether the vehicle runs 100 km or 50,000 km, for the simple reason that fixed costs are unaffected by vehicle activity.

It should be noted that transport operators tend to call *administrative* fixed costs 'establishment charges', and *vehicle* fixed costs 'standing charges'.

5.1.6 VARIABLE COSTS

Variable costs are the opposite to fixed costs and vary directly with 'mileage'. Going back to our vehicle, its variable costs (e.g. fuel, oil, tyres) increase with 'mileage'.

It should be noted that transport operators tend to call variable costs 'running costs'.

5.1.7 SEMI-FIXED COSTS

A semi-fixed cost is partly fixed and partly variable. A telephone bill, for example, is such a cost, being made up of a fixed rental and a variable charge per unit.

C

5.1.8 OVERHEADS

An overhead is essentially an indirect cost which arises from the overall business activity and is usually, but not always, of an administrative nature. Examples are directors' and office salaries, stationery, telephone charges

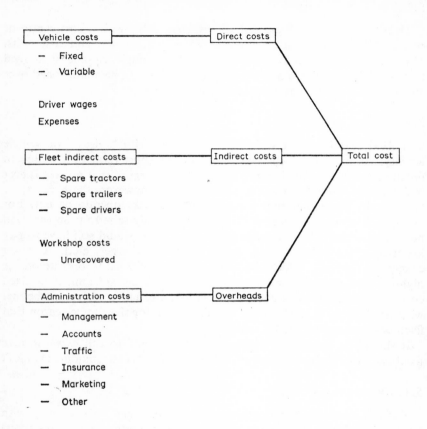

FIGURE 1. Total cost summary

and depreciation. Non-administrative overheads – or fleet overheads – comprise such items as tarpaulins, sheets, ropes, the use of spare tractors, trailers, etc. All overheads have to be taken into account when traffic rates are fixed. Figure 1 shows the breakdown of total cost under direct and indirect costs and overhead.

5.1.9 OVERHEAD ALLOCATION

From the recording point of view overheads are allocated where they fall. In a large firm, for example, there would be a number of departments such as Accounts, Estimating, Traffic, Workshop, etc., each of which would be charged with its own direct expenses, i.e. staff salaries and wages, office supplies, temporary labour, etc.; to these may be added *apportioned* expenses as described below.

5.1.10 OVERHEAD APPORTIONMENT

Overheads such as rents, rates, insurance, depreciation, etc., not incurred by a specific department or cost centre may be shared or apportioned among the departments or cost centres which they serve. There are various ways of doing this, for example:

Overhead	Basis of apportionment
Rent and rates	Floor area
Insurance	Insured values
Welfare	Number of personnel
Electricity	Number of points/kWh/ estimated consumption

In the case of the very small operator it is sufficient to aggregate overheads and recover them *en bloc* from vehicle operations.

5.1.11 OVERHEAD ABSORPTION

When overheads are charged out to vehicle cost centres and thence to cost units they are said to be *absorbed* or cleared in cost – recovered from the wheels that turn. Overheads can be absorbed in a number of ways:

1 On payload.
2 On the number of vehicles.
3 On a combination of 1 and 2.
4 On a percentage uplift on operating costs.
5 On vehicle capital values.

Overhead absorption (or *recovery*) is discussed more fully in Chapter 7.

5.2 ROAD TRANSPORT COSTS

In a road transport business costs can be grouped under three main headings: costs incurred by the vehicle, costs incurred by the driver, and overheads.

5.2.1 COSTS INCURRED BY THE VEHICLE

Vehicle costs should be separated under fixed and variable costs.

(*a*) *Vehicle Fixed Costs*

These are costs which are incurred before a vehicle is allowed to operate on the public highway; they are generally fixed for a period of one year.

Licences
Insurance
Depreciation
Rent and rates (or garaging)
Hire purchase interest
Overhead charges

It should be noted that depreciation is an annual or *time* expense and is incurred whether a vehicle runs or not, although it can be related to the number of kilometres a vehicle is expected to cover in a year. Rent and rates are incurred whether a vehicle is garaged out or on an operator's premises, according to the amount of space it occupies; whether these costs should be separated from the general business overhead or not is a policy matter for each firm to decide.

(*b*) *Vehicle variable costs*

These costs are incurred during vehicle operation.

Fuel
Oil
Tyres
Repairs and maintenance
Sundries

Although it could be argued that repairs and maintenance should be classed as a semi-fixed cost they have purposely been treated as a variable for the reasons given in Chapter 6 (section 6.2.5).

5.2.2 COSTS INCURRED BY THE DRIVER

These are the driver's wages (plus payment for any incentive scheme) including the employer's payroll contributions such as national health insurance, graduated pension, company pension scheme, etc., and a living-out or subsistence allowance.

Gross wages
Employer's payroll contributions
Company pension scheme contribution (if any)
Subsistence allowance

5.2.3 OVERHEADS

Overhead costs should be separated under fleet and business.

(a) Fleet costs

These represent costs arising from fleet operations such as *spare* tractors, trailers, and drivers, and consumable equipment such as tarpaulins, sheets, and ropes, which are apportioned over the vehicles they serve. Workshop costs also come under fleet activity but are treated as a separate entity as explained further on.

(b) Business costs

These are costs which are incurred by the general administration of the business/department and include such items as:

Salaries and fees	Cars and expenses
Rent and rates	Legal and professional fees
Light and heat	Depreciation
Insurance	Bad debts
Maintenance (premises, etc.)	Training
Telephones and telex	Bank charges
Postage and stationery	Interest (hire purchase and loan)
Subscriptions	Advertising
Travelling	Welfare
Entertaining	Other expenses

Administrative costs have no direct connection with vehicles except that they must be recovered from fleet operations.

5.3 SUMMARY

1 A cost unit is a unit in which costs are measured or expressed, e.g. the kilometre run.

2 A cost centre is a location, person, or item of equipment against which costs are charged, e.g. a vehicle, a workshop.

3 Costs are analysed in a number of ways: under direct and indirect costs; by cost centres, departments, and depots, which are further subdivided into fixed, semi-fixed, and variable costs.

4 Fixed costs do not normally vary with business activity and are usually fixed for a year, e.g. vehicle fixed and administrative costs. Variable costs vary with activity, e.g. kilometres run.

5 Overheads are indirect costs which are not wholly identifiable with, but which can be apportioned to, a cost centre or cost unit.

6 Overheads should be divided into business (or administrative) overheads and fleet overheads.

7 Overheads can be recovered (or absorbed) in a number of ways, payload and number of vehicles being the most common.

8 Road haulage costs should be grouped under three main headings: vehicle costs, driver's costs, and overheads.

6 Vehicle Costs and their Sources

We can now discuss each type of cost in more detail and state the particular source from which each is obtained.

6.1 VEHICLE FIXED COSTS

6.1.1 LICENCES

Licences include the road fund licence and carriers' licence. The carriers' licence is a nominal sum compared with the more hefty road licence, which is based on unladen weight and therefore varies from vehicle to vehicle. It is just one of the burdensome fixed costs with which transport operators have to contend and can run into hundreds of pounds per vehicle.

Source: the licensing authority.

6.1.2 INSURANCE

Insurance is another high cost which is dependent on a number of factors: area or region, type of load, special risk, number of vehicles in fleet (for discount purposes), and so on.

Source: insurance company or broker (or renewal form).

6.1.3 DEPRECIATION

The fixed costs just described are probably the simplest because they are a straight copy from a piece of paper. Depreciation is a little more difficult as it has to be calculated after the particular method to be used has been selected. There are a number of methods of computing depreciation but only two are of interest to us here: the 'straight-line' and 'reducing-balance' methods.

(a) Straight-line depreciation

This method takes the purchase price of a vehicle, *less* tyres, and writes it off over the estimated *effective life* of the vehicle.

Example:

XYZ Motor Vehicle

	£
Capital cost	3,300
less Tyres	(420)
	2,880
less Residual value	—
	2,880

To be written off over six years: £480 per annum

Tyre costs have been deducted because it would be ludicrous to write them off over six years when it is known they will have to be replaced in a year or so. (*See*, however, section 6.2.4). Residual value has been left blank. This is because no operator can be expected to estimate a realistic price or exchange value for a vehicle six years hence. He should therefore assume the worst and ignore it altogether.

(b) Reducing-balance depreciation

This method assumes that depreciation will be heavier in the early years of a vehicle's life when repairs are light, and lighter in later years when repairs become more of a burden. The object of this method is to write an asset down to its net realizable value at the end of its working life.

Example:

XYZ Motor Vehicle
Amount to be written down at 25% per annum: £2,880

		£
Initial value		2,880
less Depreciation:	Year 1	(720)
		2,160
	Year 2	(540)
		1,620
	Year 3	(405)
		1,215
	Year 4	(304)
		911
	Year 5	(230)
		681
	Year 6	(170)
Residual or book value		511

(c) Straight-line or reducing-balance method?

Of the two methods straight-line depreciation is the easier to understand and operate and is therefore to be recommended.

Some operators use the reducing-balance method in the erroneous belief that they are applying the same principle as the Inland Revenue. The belief is true where the initial allowance and writing-down allowance are the same as those laid down by the Inland Revenue *from the moment of purchase.* But even then an operator must ask himself whether the allowances are realistic. Depreciation depends upon two factors: time and use, with the emphasis on the latter. In short, depreciation rates should be based on the estimated *effective life* of a vehicle and not on a rate for taxation purposes. Type of vehicle, frequency, load, terrain, driver, and maintenance all have their effect on a vehicle's life, and an operator must take these into account when determining depreciation rates.

When fixing traffic rates there is a very good case for using inflated rates of depreciation to cover the higher cost of replacement vehicles. This is a separate issue from costing, however, and is dealt with in Chapter 10.

Source: vehicle register.

6.1.4 RENT AND RATES OR GARAGING

Charges for rent and rates are normally based on area. In a haulage firm which has an administration block, workshop, and parking area rent and rates should be apportioned on floor area. Where an administration block has a number of floors the overall area should be taken into account. The cost of rent and rates for garaging (or parking) is thus known and should be compared with what it would cost to park outside the premises. The result should show a saving even though the apportionment on area may not be 100 per cent accurate. The cost of rent and rates should be apportioned among the number of vehicles according to the amount of space each occupies when parking.

Suppose, for example, that the annual rent and rates of A. Haulier Ltd are £3,000, of which the portions applying to administration, workshop, and parking area are £1,400, £200, and £1,400 respectively, and that each of the six vehicles takes up the same amount of space, then each vehicle would be charged annually with £233.

Where a property is freehold and no rent is involved, should an operator include a nominal rent? As costing is concerned with the facts – what has actually been spent or incurred – the answer is in the negative, although there may be good reason for its inclusion when fixing traffic rates.

Source: rent and rates schedule (showing floor area of premises and sum involved).

6.1.5 HIRE PURCHASE INTEREST

When a vehicle is bought through a hire purchase company a statement (or *agreement*) is given to the purchaser showing *inter alia* the basic price, the hire purchase price, the deposit paid (or price allowed), and the number of payments which have to be made to complete the hire purchase agreement. For example:

Basic price	£3,300
Hire purchase interest	£ 412
	£3,712

A vehicle so purchased should be taken on to a firm's books at the *basic* price (the Vehicle Asset account being charged with £3,300 and a Hire Purchase Interest Expense account with £412) and the interest written off over the term of the hire purchase agreement. If, for example, the term was two years, then the sum of £206 would be added to the vehicle's fixed costs at the commencement of the year.

Source: hire purchase agreement or vehicle register.

6.1.6 OVERHEAD CHARGES

As already explained, overheads should be separated into fleet costs and business costs. The former are those involved as the result of fleet operations while the latter are the result of the general administration of the business. These are dealt with separately in Chapter 7.

Source: nominal ledger analysis.

6.2 VEHICLE VARIABLE COSTS

6.2.1 FUEL

Fuel is the most significant variable cost. If it is not then there is something wrong. It is significant because:

1 It contains a high tax content.
2 The fuel consumption of most vehicles, other than lightweight vehicles, has a low k.p.l.

Above-average fuel consumption can be due to a number of factors: poor maintenance, a worn engine, a heavy foot, vehicle overladen, tyres under-inflated, and so on. Whatever the cause it should be traced and rectified if the cost is to be kept to a minimum. Individual vehicle cost sheets are an excellent guide to fuel control (*see* Figure 16), but where such records are not kept it is strongly recommended that consumption figures are ascertained from either a driver's log sheet (which show *inter alia* fuel issued and kilometres run) or his record sheet (*see* Figure 9), for comparison with the accepted average consumption of a particular vehicle.

Booking errors can be a source of annoyance – i.e. a supply of fuel booked against the wrong vehicle – as they immediately show up as excess consumption. Investigation of heavy fuel consumption should therefore begin with fuel issue sheets rather than the vehicle itself.

Fuel stock control is dealt with in Chapter 9.

Source: fuel and oil issue sheets (*see* Figure 10).

6.2.2 OIL

Although engine oil is the smallest variable cost its consumption should nevertheless be carefully watched. So long as a vehicle is being carefully driven and maintained there should not be any sharp rise in consumption per kilometre. If the fuel and oil records show the contrary then an investigation should be made to ensure that the apparent excess consumption is not due to some clerical error whereby a vehicle has been incorrectly charged with a supply of oil. Getting a driver to sign for oil receipts, after he has checked the quantity, should eradicate errors of this kind. If there are no clerical errors then excessive fuel consumption might mean a job for the workshop. Oil should, of course, be bought in bulk – so long as there is adequate storage space and security – in order to obtain bulk discounts.

Source: fuel and oil issue sheets (*see* Figure 10).

6.2.3 TYRES

As already intimated, tyre costs should be deducted from a vehicle's capital cost before depreciation is calculated. This is because most tyres have to be replaced within a year or so, and it is right and proper that tyre usage is recorded under variable costs.

The procedure is to take the total cost of a full set of tyres (excluding the spare) and divide it by the estimated tyre life in order to arrive at a cost per kilometre. As an example:

Example:

8-wheeled vehicle: tyres cost £40 each
Estimated tyre life: 40,000 km

$$\therefore \text{Tyre cost per kilometre: } \frac{£320}{40,000} = £0.80 \text{ per km}$$

For every kilometre run a charge of £0·008 would be made on the vehicle's cost sheet (*see* example in Chapter 9 (section 9.6)).

To be realistic, however, proper tyre records should be maintained so that in the event of excessive wear or a blow-out an adjustment can be made on the cost sheet after allowing for the cost previously charged. For example, if one of the above tyres became useless after 7,000 km and the *individual* tyre rate was £0·001 per km (i.e. £40 ÷ 40,000 km), the adjustment would be £33, calculated as follows:

Cost of tyre	£40
less 7,000 run at £0·001 per km	(£7)
Amount to be written off	£33

FIGURE 2. Tyre record (1).

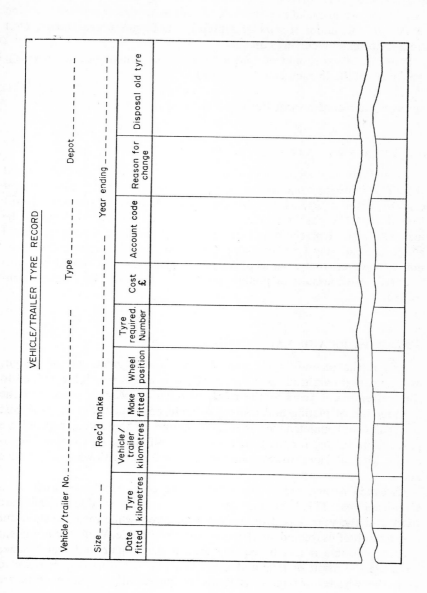

FIGURE 3. Tyre record (2).

It should be noted that tyre costs are kept separate from repair and maintenance costs for the very reason that they are *known* or expected costs. Repair and maintenance costs are unpredictable (except for routine servicing), and major repairs or replacements (engines, gear boxes, etc.) are not normally recurring costs.

Tubes and flaps should of course be included with tyre costs providing the length of life in each case is the same.

Source: tyre record or schedule (*see* Figures 2 and 3).

6.2.4 TYRES AS PART OF CAPITAL COST

There is an argument for treating tyres as part of a vehicle's capital cost. This is because a vehicle cannot run without tyres any more than it can run without an engine and, apart from blow-outs, the annual cost should be fairly constant. The annual cost of tyres could therefore be included with depreciation. This treatment would also reduce clerical effort in computing tyre costs and maintaining tyre records. It should be noted, however, that a large operator's annual tyre costs could run into hundreds of thousands of pounds and should therefore be carefully controlled.

6.2.5 REPAIRS AND MAINTENANCE

This is the second-largest variable cost and is made up of labour, materials, and overheads (*see* Figure 15). It is a cost which has tended to climb over recent years as the result of inflation, wage awards, and the introduction of plating and testing. It could be argued that the true cost of repairs and maintenance is a combination of the actual expenditure plus the profit lost for the time a vehicle is off the road. Costing is concerned with the facts, however (i.e. actual costs), not with what might have been.

As stated earlier, repair and maintenance costs can be regarded as a semi-fixed cost. This is because certain costs such as routine servicing are fixed over the year (based on annual kilometres) while repair costs occur as the result of usage and are therefore strictly variable. While the argument sounds plausible it can be equally argued that repair and maintenance costs are the result of *time* and *usage* and that the workshop is there to keep the wheels turning. It is therefore suggested that these costs are treated collectively as variable.

The cumulative amounts shown under repairs and maintenance on a vehicle cost sheet over a period of time could well determine whether or not the same type or make of vehicle should be purchased again.

A programme of preventive maintenance is an excellent way of reducing repair costs and enhancing resale value.

Sources: labour, time sheet; *materials,* parts requisition; *overheads,* overhead analysis; *outside repairs,* invoices.

6.2.6 SUNDRIES

Sundries include such items as bridge and ferry tolls, parking, and so on.

Source: driver's expense sheet.

6.3 DRIVER COSTS

6.3.1 WAGES AND RELATED PAYROLL COSTS

Having dealt with vehicle costs we now come to those costs incurred by the driver. Whether driver wages should be regarded as a fixed or variable cost is a matter of opinion. One accountant might readily treat wages as a variable; another might treat the basic wage as fixed and any overtime as a variable; while a third might treat wages as fixed on the basis that they are tending to become more and more fixed – i.e. driving hours limited to ten a day, on top of which firms do not readily stand off drivers who are already in short supply. The label is unimportant, but in view of the high cost of wages it is recommended that they be treated quite separately from vehicle costs, just the same as overheads.

Wages include, of course, overtime and bonus payments (if any), and employer's payroll contributions such as national health insurance, graduated pension, etc., which are direct charges. But just how direct is dependent on the size and complexity of fleet operations. In the case of a small operator who employs few vehicles there should be no problem, as more often than not each driver is allocated a particular vehicle; and even if he does drive other vehicles during the week the wages clerk can easily allocate his wages from his time sheet, so that each vehicle is properly charged. In a large firm with numerous vehicles where drivers transfer from vehicle to vehicle, the wages analysis can be an extremely difficult task, in which case it might be more expedient to use either standard or average driver rates. In this way the clerical task would be simplified, but reconciliation between what is paid out and what is shown on the vehicle costs sheets is most important. The answer to the problem is, of course, to stop drivers transferring from vehicle to vehicle, which is really a management problem.

The importance of keeping proper time sheets cannot be overstressed as fictitious wage costs would affect individual vehicle profit statements and therefore mislead management. Whether the back of the driver's official log book or a separate time sheet is used for this purpose does not matter so long as the recordings are accurate.

Source: payroll analysis (or time sheets)/standard rates schedule.

6.3.2 DRIVER'S SUBSISTENCE

Subsistence or lodging allowance for overnight stops can be paid as a reimbursement on the receipt of a bill or as a fixed sum per night. The latter method is to be preferred as it is simpler to operate and perhaps more fair to the driver who would otherwise have to use his own money until he returned to his depot. It is not uncommon therefore for a driver to collect his subsistence allowance from a cashier in advance of a journey.

Source: driver's expense sheet (or petty-cash analysis).

6.4 SUMMARY

1 Vehicle fixed costs comprise licences, insurance, depreciation, rent and rates (or garaging), hire purchase interest (if any), and overhead charges.
2 There are at least two methods of computing depreciation, the straight-line and reducing-balance methods being the most common.
3 Vehicle variable costs comprise fuel, oil, tyres, repairs and maintenance, and sundry expenses such as tolls and parking.
4 Tyre costs can be treated as either a variable cost or as part of capital cost.
5 Repair and maintenance costs, although partly fixed and partly variable, are more easily treated as variable costs.
6 Driver's wages include overtime, bonus payments, and employer payroll contributions. In view of the high cost of wages it is advisable to separate them from other costs.

7 Overheads and their Absorption

It has been explained earlier that there are two kinds of overheads with which an operator has to contend: *fleet* and *business* overheads. In a small firm it is highly probable that the former do not arise because with a small number of vehicles an operator is able to charge out each expense direct against a vehicle. In firms with large fleets, however, the problem can be a real one if costing is to mean anything.

7.1 ABSORPTION AND RECOVERY

Although in practice there is a certain laxity in the use of the term 'overhead recovery', it is usual for accountants to distinguish two terms:

(a) Overhead absorption

This means charging the costs to operations, vehicles or 'job'. Thus workshop overhead costs may be charged out at £x per hour and this is the absorption rate. For estimating purposes a predetermined rate would be used.

(b) Overhead recovery

Although often used to mean the same as absorption, in the most correct form it means ensuring that an appropriate amount of overhead cost is recovered in the price charged to customers.

This distinction may appear academic, but in fact is of vital importance in understanding the nature of cost accounting.

7.2 INDIRECT FLEET COSTS

These include *spare* tractors, trailers, and drivers, also tarpaulins, sheets, and ropes, but *not* workshop costs which, as we shall see later, are a direct charge against vehicles.

7.2.1 SPARE TRACTORS

These are used both for shunting and on the road as the occasion demands. The costs involved are:

Road fund licence
Insurance
Depreciation
Rent and rates
Hire purchase interest (if any)
Repairs and maintenance
Fuel and oil
Tyres

Each fixed and variable cost should be separately listed under tractor number or registration. 'Yard' fuel, oil, and tyres would have to be estimated for the financial year in order to be recovered from fleet operations.

7.2.2 SPARE TRAILERS

The ratio of trailers to tractors is dependent on the nature of a business. The average operator might have three to two, while a haulier who hires out trailers as a source of revenue might have a much higher ratio. The costs involved are:

Insurance
Depreciation
Rent and rates
Hire purchase interest (if any)
Repairs and maintenance
Tyres

It is stressed again that whether rent and rates are included for tractors and trailers is a matter for management to decide. Each expense should be listed under trailer number. Variable expenses should be estimated for the financial year.

7.2.3 SPARE DRIVERS

Spare drivers' wages can be totalled *en bloc*. If a driver is only 'spare' for, say, half of the year – the other half being spent on the road – then only half of his wages should be included as a fleet overhead. By 'spare' we mean: over and above normal on the road requirements but necessary for 'at home' duties plus any contingency that may arise (e.g. sickness, holidays, breakdown). The costs included are:

Gross wages (or a proportion thereof)
Employer's payroll contributions
Company pension scheme contributions (if any)

7.2.4 APPORTIONMENT OF 'SPARES' COSTS

Fleet 'spares' should be apportioned to vehicles according to the number they serve. As the ratio in each case may vary, three separate apportionments may be necessary. This is usually a once-a-year job which is not very time-consuming (*see* Figure 4).

FLEET SPARES APPORTIONMENT SUMMARY	Tractors	Trailers	Drivers
Number	X	X	X
	£	£	£
Licence	X	X	
Insurance	X	X	
Depreciation	X	X	
Rent and rates	X	X	
Hire purchase interest	X	X	
Repairs and maintenance	X	X	
Fuel and oil	X		
Tyres	X	X	
Wages			X
Other costs	X	X	X
Total cost	X	X	X
Units served	X	X	X
Cost per unit	£X	£X	£X

FIGURE 4. Fleet spares apportionment summary.

Example:

5 *spare tractors*
 Annual costs (fixed and variable): £3,000
 Number of units served: 40
 Share per unit: £75
20 *spare trailers*
 Annual costs (fixed and variable): £2,400
 Number of units served: 40
 Share per unit: £60
5 *spare drivers*
 Annual cost: £4,000
 Number of units served: 40
 Share per unit: £100

In this example the imaginary company has 45 tractors, 60 trailers, and 45 drivers. Each vehicle would therefore be charged with an additional annual cost of £235 which would form part of the total vehicle fixed cost.

Important note: The treatment for arriving at a realistic rate where trailers are regularly hired out on a commercial basis is discussed in Chapter 10.

7.2.5 TARPAULINS, SHEETS, AND ROPES

Tarpaulins and sheets are very often transferred from vehicle to vehicle (sometimes to other operators' vehicles!) while ropes either wear out or disappear. In a small firm the problem is a minor one as each vehicle normally has its own set which stays with the vehicle. But in medium and large undertakings the problem can be very acute and costly.

A way of ensuring that each vehicle is properly charged with its fair share of the cost is to assume that each vehicle has its own standard set (as applicable to each *type* of vehicle), estimate the life of each item, and allocate to each vehicle on a cost per annum basis. If a tarpaulin is stolen or lost any remaining value which has not been included in the costing records should be written off in the accounts.

The question that must now be asked is whether these costs should be treated as fixed or variable. Here again there are arguments for and against. As far as the administration of a costing system is concerned it is preferable to treat them as fixed and group them with the other indirect costs. Some operators, however, charge out sheets and ropes as a direct cost.

7.3 BUSINESS OVERHEADS

7.3.1 ADMINISTRATIVE EXPENSES

A list of overhead expenses has been given in Chapter 6. The list is by no means exhaustive and every operator knows to his cost the extent to which these expenses have risen in recent years, particularly rates and telephone and postal charges.

Albeit these are the costs of being in business, and so long as they are controlled and the correct traffic rates are used, an operator should not worry himself unduly. Controlling them is important but not to the extent of being penny wise, pound foolish. As we saw in Chapter 4, if A. Haulier Ltd had increased his payroll by investing in a costing clerk, the costing information produced could have increased profit by £2,000 if the information had been properly used.

It should be stated here that business overheads are those expenses remaining after all other costs and expenses have been allocated and/or apportioned. For example, when rent and rates have been apportioned to fleet parking and workshop, what is left can be truly regarded as an administrative expense.

7.3.2 OVERHEAD DISTRIBUTION SUMMARY

To ensure that costs are properly allocated and apportioned an overhead distribution summary should be drawn up, as in Figure 5.

7.3.3 APPORTIONMENT OF OVERHEADS

The apportionment of business overheads to vehicles should not be a slap-dash affair as though it were something unimportant. Like all costing it should be as accurate and sensible as possible if the facts are to be presented. How, then, should overheads be apportioned?

There are several ways in which this can be done and it is a matter of selecting the most appropriate method. Possible bases for apportionment are:

1 Number of vehicles.
2 Potential payload.
3 Combination of methods 1 and 2.
4 Percentage uplift on operating costs.
5 Vehicle capital values.

Methods 4 and 5 are not recommended. Among the firms that operate a costing system method 1 is fairly common. Own-account operators who do not carry for reward may find it useful but not necessarily accurate if they require sound costing information. But when identical or similar vehicles are employed it is the obvious and easiest choice.

OVERHEAD DISTRIBUTION SUMMARY— YEAR ENDED 19---

	(1) Basis	(2) Total £	(3) Fleet £	(4) Workshop £	(5) Warehouse £	(6) Administration £	(7) Traffic £	(8) Accounts £	(9) General £
Salaries and wages	Direct								
Rent and rates	Area								
Light and heat	HWH loading								
Licences	Direct								
Insurance	Values								
Repairs and maintenance	Direct								
Telephones and telex	Estimates								
Postage and stationery	Direct								
Subscriptions	Direct								
Travelling	Direct								
Entertaining	Direct								
Cars and expenses	Direct								
Legal and professional	Direct								
Depreciation	Direct								
Bad debts	Direct								
Training	Direct								
Bank charges	Direct								
Hire purchase interest	Direct								
Advertising	Direct								
Welfare	Direct								
Other expenses	Various								
Indirect materials	Direct								
Total departmental overheads									

1 The basis of allocation/apportionment is shown in column (1) and the total of each cost/expense in column (2).
2 Administration costs (column 6) are further divided in columns (7)–(9) under traffic, accounts, and general.
3 The summary shows at a glance the overheads applicable to each department and section.
4 Indirect materials includes items such as: tarpaulins, sheets, ropes, yard fuel, etc. (fleet); grease, rags, etc. (workshop); office-cleaning materials, etc. (administration); and so on.
5 Vehicle direct costs (fixed and variable) and driver costs are not shown in the summary (except for rent and rates) whereas all fleet indirect costs are,

FIGURE 5. Overhead distribution summary.

(a) Number-of-vehicles basis

If we invent a small company we can see how this works. Suppose a company's fleet has the following vehicles:

```
2 vehicles, 20 tonnes each
3      „    15    „    „
3      „    10    „    „
4      „     7    „    „
```

(Tonnes refer to carrying capacity and not, of course, to overall weight.) If the business overhead is, say, £6,000 the annual sum to be charged to each vehicle is £500, that is:

$$£6,000 \div 12 = £500$$

If all twelve vehicles were of the same type, class, and capacity this basis would be recommended. But as profitability is normally based on capacity – i.e. large vehicles carry more traffic than smaller ones and therefore earn more revenue – it may be more equitable to apportion overheads on payload rather than the number of vehicles. As stated above, where payloads are similar there is no problem; but where they differ, as in this example, the payload basis should be used.

(b) Potential-payload basis

The computation is as follows:

```
 2 vehicles, 20 tonnes each = 40 tonnes
 3      „    15    „    „    = 45    „
 3      „    10    „    „    = 30    „
 4      „     7    „    „    = 28    „
──                            ───
12                            143
══                            ═══
```

$$£6,000 \div 143 \text{ tonnes} = £41 \cdot 96 \text{ per tonne}$$

If the payload is rounded to £42 the calculation is:

```
20-tonne vehicles: 20 × £42 = £840
15      „        „  15 × £42 = £630
10      „        „  10 × £42 = £420
 7      „        „   7 × £42 = £294
```

Proof of calculation:

```
                                              £
2 vehicles 20 tonnes each (2 × £840)   1,680
2      „   15    „      „  (3 × £630)   1,890
3      „   10    „      „  (3 × £420)   1,260
4      „    7    „      „  (4 × £294)   1,176
                                       ─────
                                       6,006
                                       ═════
```

(*Note*: the difference of £6 is due to rounding.) The two largest revenue-earning vehicles are thus charged with an annual overhead of £840 each, while the smallest revenue-earning vehicles are charged with £294 each.

It can be argued that the business overhead is the same regardless of the fleet payload, in which case the number-of-vehicles basis might be preferred, besides being a less cumbersome exercise. The point to bear in mind, however, is that the apportionment of overheads should be as realistic and fair as possible if management are to act on the information presented. Moreover, where basic costing information is incorporated in rate fixing calculations it should be as reliable as possible; to burden a 7-tonne vehicle with the same amount of overhead as a 20-tonne vehicle, for example, could easily lead to overpricing and therefore loss of traffic as rates would obviously be higher for the 7-tonne vehicle. The payload basis is therefore to be recommended.

(c) *Number/payload basis*

Some schools of thought favour a combination of these methods whereby half (£3,000) of the business overhead is apportioned on the number of vehicles and the other half (£3,000) on payload. Figure 6 shows the outcome of all *three* methods. The number/payload basis is really a compromise and can therefore be discounted.

(d) *Apportionment rules*

The rules derived from what has been said so far can be summarized as follows:

1 Apportion overheads on the number of vehicles when vehicles have similar payloads.
2 Apportion overheads on fleet payload when payloads vary among vehicles.

(e) *Other bases*

What has been said so far applies to the general type of operator who carries a variety of goods from A to B. For the more specialized type of operator a different type of apportionment may be necessary. For example, a haulier whose fleet specializes in the movement of wide loads might apportion his overheads on a time basis according to the working schedule of each vehicle. Each operator should decide the method most suitable for his type of business.

OVERHEAD ABSORPTION SUMMARY – YEAR ENDED 19___

Vehicle number	Type	Location	Payload (Tonnes)	OVERHEAD RECOVERY METHOD AND RATE PER ANNUM			CALCULATIONS		
				(1) Number £	(2) Payload £	(3) No./Payload £	(1) Number £	(2) Payload £	(3) No./Payload £
1	XY	London	20	500	839	670	$\frac{6\,000}{12}$	$6\,000 \times \frac{20}{143}$	$\frac{1}{2}$ No. $+ \frac{1}{2}$ PL
2	XY	Rugby	20	500	839	670	$\frac{6\,000}{12}$	$6\,000 \times \frac{20}{143}$	$\frac{1}{2}$ No. $+ \frac{1}{2}$ PL
3	AB	London	15	500	629	564	$\frac{6\,000}{12}$	$6\,000 \times \frac{15}{143}$	$\frac{1}{2}$ No. $+ \frac{1}{2}$ PL
4	AB	Rugby	15	500	629	564	$\frac{6\,000}{12}$	$6\,000 \times \frac{15}{143}$	$\frac{1}{2}$ No. $+ \frac{1}{2}$ PL
5	AC	Ashford	15	500	629	564	$\frac{6\,000}{12}$	$6\,000 \times \frac{15}{143}$	$\frac{1}{2}$ No. $+ \frac{1}{2}$ PL
6	FP	London	10	500	419	460	$\frac{6\,000}{12}$	$6\,000 \times \frac{10}{143}$	$\frac{1}{2}$ No. $+ \frac{1}{2}$ PL
7	FP	Rugby	10	500	420	460	$\frac{6\,000}{12}$	$6\,000 \times \frac{10}{143}$	$\frac{1}{2}$ No. $+ \frac{1}{2}$ PL
8	FT	Ashford	10	500	420	460	$\frac{6\,000}{12}$	$6\,000 \times \frac{10}{143}$	$\frac{1}{2}$ No. $+ \frac{1}{2}$ PL
9	Z1	London	7	500	294	397	$\frac{6\,000}{12}$	$6\,000 \times \frac{7}{143}$	$\frac{1}{2}$ No. $+ \frac{1}{2}$ PL
10	Z1	London	7	·500	294	397	$\frac{6\,000}{12}$	$6\,000 \times \frac{7}{143}$	$\frac{1}{2}$ No. $+ \frac{1}{2}$ PL
11	Z2	Rugby	7	500	294	397	$\frac{6\,000}{12}$	$6\,000 \times \frac{7}{143}$	$\frac{1}{2}$ No. $+ \frac{1}{2}$ PL
12	Z2	Ashford	7	500	294	397	$\frac{6\,000}{12}$	$6\,000 \times \frac{7}{143}$	$\frac{1}{2}$ No. $+ \frac{1}{2}$ PL
Total			143	6 000	6 000	6 000			

FIGURE 6 Overhead absorption summary

Note: Other methods of recovery could be incorporated as necessary. The objective of the exercise is to show management the alternative methods available and their effect on vehicle traffic rates.

7.3.4 OVERHEAD ABSORPTION AND RECOVERY

Once overheads have been apportioned to vehicles, they are ultimately charged out to fleet operations. If they are not fully recovered in the rates charged the result will be a diminution in profit or perhaps a loss. Here again we must stress the importance of good estimating which ensures that all costs are adequately covered and that the profit loading is both reasonable to the firm and acceptable to the customer.

When hauliers foolishly follow the practice of copying other hauliers' rates less a small reduction, they do not realize the threat that it can have on their business. The subject is discussed in Chapter 10 but it can be said here that no two firms are alike. Overheads vary from firm to firm and it is quite foolish to price according to another firm's overhead structure. More often than not that other firm has already copied some other haulier's rates and in turn has reduced them slightly. So long as the 'copied' rates cover a firm's costs and generate sufficient profit there is no real problem. But as most haulage firms are not aware whether this is so or not until their accountant has prepared their annual accounts – perhaps some four to six months after the year end – there is the very grave danger of their incurring a deficit on the profit-and-loss account.

The time has now arrived when every operator should stand on his own two feet, know his own costs, fix his own prices, and compete in a proper manner.

7.4 SUMMARY

1 Overheads should be divided into *fleet* overheads (including spare tractors, trailers, and drivers and tarpaulins, sheets, and ropes – except in the latter case where these can be charged direct) and *business* overheads (including staff salaries, office costs, etc.).
2 An overhead distribution summary should be drawn up and cover all fleet and business overheads.
3 The cost of spare tractors, trailers, and drivers should be apportioned over the vehicles they serve; the cost of tarpaulins, sheets, and ropes should be charged to vehicles on the assumption that each vehicle has its own permanent set.
4 Business overheads should be apportioned to vehicles on the basis of the number of vehicles where they are similar in type and payload; and on the basis of payload where vehicles and payloads differ.
5 Other methods of overhead absorption might apply according to the type of business or traffic concerned.
6 Overheads are recovered from fleet operations by their inclusion in traffic rates.

Workshop Costs and their Absorption

.1 METHODS OF COSTING

Although costing is not at present widely used in transport operations it is nevertheless applied in some form to workshop activities, possibly because is a relatively simple affair in this context. Even so, the methods employed re somewhat crude and include the following:

Material plus labour costs.
As method 1 plus xp per hour to cover overheads.
Materials plus the rate charged by the local garage to cover labour and overheads.

With the exception of method 1 such practice is foolish to say the least, and tantamount to playing with figures.

2 THE WORKSHOP AS A COST CENTRE

workshop should be treated as a cost centre. A mature management ould want to know:

The cost of running a workshop.
The purpose it serves.
Whether or not it is cheaper to subcontract all repair work.

o say glibly that the workshop is there to serve the company's fleet of hicles is no answer at all. The answer must be quantified in terms of cost vings.

3 WORKSHOP COSTS

he first task is to determine the annual cost of running a workshop. orkshop costs are normally straightforward and include: wages and pay- ll costs; depreciation (premises and equipment); insurance; repairs and aintenance; light, heat, and power; rent and rates; welfare and other ff costs; and sundries.

A method of analysing each of these costs is *via* the overhead distributio
summary shown in Figure 5. Costs are obtained as follows:

1 *Wages and payroll costs*: number of fitters (plus other workshop staff,
any), annual gross pay for each plus employer's contributions. If over
time is a regular feature an estimate should be made at the full rate.
2 *Depreciation*: taken direct from the plant register. (If no such record
available obtain figure from firm's auditors, or estimate.)
3 *Insurance*: from insurance register or renewal receipts. (In case of diff
culty consult firm's insurance broker.)
4 *Repairs and maintenance*: estimate annual cost of expected repairs an
maintenance.
5 *Light, heat, and power*: as no separate meters are likely to be availabl
estimate annual cost, taking into account the number of lamps and th
on/off time, power tool loads and utilization, winter heating, and so o
6 *Rent and rates*: floor area.
7 *Welfare*: paid benefits received by the staff (e.g. overall service, refresh
ments). Other staff costs would include staff advertising, etc.
8 *Sundries*: consumable items such as lamps, grease, hand cleaner, an
sundry expenses.

A projected workshop cost schedule might appear as below

Example:

Projected Workshop Costs for the year ended 19..
£

Wages, etc.*	3,000
Depreciation	300
Insurance	20
Repairs	80
Light and heat	100
Rent and rates	800
Welfare	50
Sundries	50
	4,400

(* three fitters, no other staff; although included
here to obtain an overall rate some accountants
would prefer an absorption rate which excluded
wages)

8.4 UTILIZATION

The next step is to ascertain the average time utilized by workshop st
on repair and maintenance work. This could be obtained by analysi
fitters' time sheets over a period of time (e.g. six months), but a better w

vould be to take each fitter's annual time available and eliminate all
expected non-productive time.

Example:

f a 42-hour week was worked throughout the year the position might be as
ollows:

A. Spanner, Workshop Fitter

otal annual hours available	2,184	(52 × 42)
ess Annual and bank holidays	168	(4 × 42)
Tea breaks	96	(2 hours per week for 48 weeks)
Contingency for idle time and sickness (10%)	192	(2,184 − 264 = 1,920)
Total expected non-productive hours	456	(456)
Productive hours available		1,728

$$\text{Utilization} = \frac{1,728}{2,184} \times 100 = 79\%$$

f the workshop employed *three* fitters the total productive hours available
ould be 5, 184 per annum.

.5 RATE PER HOUR (Composite absorption rate)

)nce we have calculated the annual cost of operating a workshop – which
y itself tells us nothing except the sum involved – the next step is to compute
cost rate per hour which will cover all expenses including wages but not,
f course, the cost of the materials used in repair and service work.
  Using the above figures the calculation is simply:

$$£4,400 \div 5,184 = £0 \cdot 809 \text{ (or 81p)}$$

or all repair and service work the sum of 81p per hour would be charged
lus the cost of materials and outside services, if any.
  By comparing a firm's own workshop rate with outside rates it should be
ear whether or not the workshop is paying for itself. Outside rates include
1 element for profit which, coupled with the inconvenience of an operator
aving to wait for outside service, makes operating one's own workshop
1 attractive proposition. There is also the added advantage of purchasing
aterials at trade prices, thus reducing repair and maintenance costs even
rther. Annual workshop 'profit' can be ascertained as follows:

Annual effective hours employed (i.e. on jobs) × average outside rate
less Annual effective hours employed (i.e. on jobs) × workshop rate
Gross profit
less Workshop overheads under-absorbed (or *plus* over-absorbed)
Net cost savings

8.6 SPARE CAPACITY

Where there is spare capacity – i.e. where labour and plant are not fully utilized, after allowance has been made for holidays, sickness, etc. – the situation could be exploited, perhaps on a temporary basis, by taking on work for other operators or businesses. In this case a figure for profit must be added to the cost rate and also to the parts used.

8.7 CONTROL INFORMATION

Costing information in terms of utilization and total charges to date is necessary to ensure that workshop costs are being recovered according to plan. The cost statement in Figure 7 shows actual expenses against forecast.

WORKSHOP COST STATEMENT – MONTH ENDED‗‗‗‗‗‗					
	MONTH		CUMULATIVE		
	Forecast £	Actual £	Forecast £	Actual £	Variance Over/(Under) £
EXPENSES:					
Wages					
Depreciation					
Insurance					
Repairs					
Light and heat					
Rent and rates					
Welfare					
Sundries					
Other					
TOTAL					
EXPENSES RECOVERED* (*Hours x rate)					
NET COST					
Hours utilized					
%					

FIGURE 7. Workshop cost statement.

expenses and actual hours absorbed from workshop activity against those forecast. The aim should be to reduce the workshop net operating cost (i.e. the expenses under-absorbed) to nil by working to full capacity and/or reducing workshop costs.

8.8 SUMMARY

1 The object of workshop costing is to ensure that workshop costs are correctly charged and that the workshop is run as an economic unit and therefore shows cost savings over outside charges.
2 The workshop should be treated as a cost centre and projected annual operating expenses should be drawn up on a workshop cost statement.
3 Workshop capacity in terms of net labour hours should be computed and divided into the total cost in order to arrive at a cost rate per hour. The rate should be compared with outside charges in order to determine the cost savings.
4 Workshop 'profit' (or net cost savings) can be determined by extending the net hours utilized over the year at the differential cost rate (i.e. the average external rate less the workshop rate) less the workshop expenses unrecovered.
5 The regular presentation of control information is important if costs are to be controlled and efficiency enhanced.

9 A Costing System in Practice

So far costing has been discussed in principle only, i.e. cost ascertainment, allocation, apportionment, and absorption. We now come to the actual recording of costing data for the guidance of management.

9.1 FORMS TO BE USED

Accumulating road transport costs from the various sources is not a haphazard affair resulting in untidy figures on the back of an envelope. Each type of cost is recorded in a proper manner on a form designed for that purpose. Specimen costing forms are outlined below; they can be used for almost any size firm, and modified where necessary to suit the particular needs of a business. The forms that would be used in an average business are:

1 Driver's daily record sheet (or reverse side of log sheet), incorporating time sheet and consignment details.
2 Vehicle record sheet.
3 Fuel and oil issue sheet.
4 Repair and maintenance record, incorporating:
   (a) Fitter's time sheet.
   (b) Parts requisition.
   (c) Vehicle repair cost sheet.
5 Vehicle cost sheet.
6 Fleet cost-and-profit statement.

9.2 DAILY RECORD SHEET

Although of a statistical nature the daily record sheet (see Figure 8) nevertheless a basic costing form in that it provides details of each job contract, e.g. goods carried, weight, destination, time taken, kilometre run, and fuel and oil used. Should the need arise it is thus possible to co each job or contract, e.g. where losses are to be traced or exception profits pinpointed. The record sheet is filled out daily by each driver an

DAILY RECORD SHEET

VEHICLE No. ------------- WEEK ENDING -----------

Day	Job No.	km reading	km run	Tonnes carried	Drops made	Hours worked	Destination	Fuel		Oil (litres)	Expenses
								Bulk (litres)	Agency (litres)		
Sunday											
Monday											
Tuesday											
Wednesday											
Thursday											
Friday											
Saturday											

Details of repairs on road etc.:

Driver's signature --------------

Note: The recorded details would vary from firm to firm, but should incorporate the requirements of the Transport Act 1968 regarding driver's hours, etc.

FIGURE 8. Daily record sheet.

D

VEHICLE RECORD SHEET

REGISTRATION No._____   MONTH ENDING._____

Day	km run	Time taken	Tonnes carried	Drops made	Fuel		Oil	Wages	Expenses	Revenue
					Bulk	Agency				
1										
2										
3										
4										
5										
6										
7										
8										
9										
10										
11										
12										
13										
14										
15										
16										
17										
18										
19										
20										
21										
22										
23										
24										
25										
26										
27										
28										
29										
30										
31										

FIGURE 9. Vehicle record sheet.

the details are summarized by a clerk on a vehicle record sheet, usually at the close of each week.

9.3 VEHICLE RECORD SHEET

The details shown on the daily record sheets are summarized daily or weekly on the vehicle record sheet (*see* Figure 9). At the close of each accounting period each vehicle's totals are transferred from the vehicle record sheet to the vehicle cost sheet, shown in Figure 16. Drivers' wages and expenses which are analysed weekly should also be shown on the vehicle record sheet (as a weekly figure) for posting to the vehicle cost sheet.

FUEL AND OIL ISSUE SHEET

DEPOT _____   DATE _____

PUMP _____

Vehicle Reg. No.	Speedo. reading	Pump reading	Diesel	Petrol	Engine	Gearbox	Diff.	Driver's signature

FIGURE 10. Fuel and oil issue sheet (1).

9.4 FUEL AND OIL RECORDS

9.4.1 FUEL AND OIL ISSUE SHEET

Two forms are shown: the first is common and is used for *all* vehicles; the second is for individual vehicles and dispenses with the task of having to analyse the first form by vehicles (*see* Figures 10 and 11).

The procedure is to issue fuel and oil as required, for which each driver

Fuel Reconciliation

	Litres	£	p
Opening stock (previous dip)			
Deliveries			
less Issues (per dockets)			
Balance			
less Closing dip			
Difference			

FIGURE 11. Fuel and oil issue sheet (2).

signs after having verified the amounts issued. At the end of each week the quantities of fuel and oil issued are summarized by vehicles and extended at the respective rates so that weekly fuel and oil costs are obtained. The quantities should be compared with the quantities recorded on the vehicle record sheets. At the accounting period end (which might be a calendar month or a four week period) the weekly amounts are totalled and tranferred to the respective vehicle cost sheets.

Small firms can probably dispense with the fuel and oil issue sheet and use the daily record sheets instead. When both forms are used, however, there is a positive check, one against the other.

9.4.2 FUEL STOCK RECONCILIATION

At this point it is prudent to mention that, if stock control is to be enhanced, fuel stocks should be balanced either daily or at least weekly, depending on the volume of issues and whether a shift system is worked.

The procedure is to take the opening balance of fuel, add purchases (or deliveries), deduct issues, and compare the balance with what is actually left in the tank, as described below:

1 *Opening stock*, which is the closing stock for the previous period (i.e. shift, day, week, or month) and has been physically measured,

plus

2 *Deliveries* from oil companies, which should be verified by a firm's employee before the suppliers' goods received notes are signed,

less

3 *Issues*, which are taken from the issue sheets (and have been checked and signed for by drivers),

leaves

4 *Balance*, which should be supported by physical measurement (e.g. tank dip).

In theory the balance by deduction and the physical (or actual) balance should agree; in practice this is seldom the case due to a number of reasons, e.g. seepage, pilferage, clerical errors. Whatever the cause it is important that the difference is obtained:

1 For writing off in the financial accounts.
2 For sponsoring management action to minimize further stock differences.

The same principle applies to oil stock.

9.4.3 AGENCY FUEL, ETC.

Purchases on the road should be analysed by vehicles from the suppliers' invoices, and the monthly or four weekly totals transferred to the respective vehicle cost sheets.

9.5 REPAIR AND MAINTENANCE RECORDS

9.5.1 WORKSHOP TIME SHEET

The form records how a fitter's paid time has been spent during the week and includes such analysis as 'waiting for parts', 'no work', etc. (*see* Figure 12). Where vehicles have been worked upon each vehicle number or

WORKSHOP TIME SHEET

NAME ------------ CLOCK No. ----------- WEEK ENDING -----------

Tractor/ trailer No.	Work done (Give details, including waiting time, etc.)	Job No.	Time taken (hr) (min)	Cost rate (Labour and overheads)	£	p
Approved by: (Foreman)						

FIGURE 12. Workshop time sheet.

registration number is recorded alongside a description of the work done and the time taken. The total hours recorded against vehicles are extended at the *cost* rate, as discussed in Chapter 8, and transferred to the respective vehicle repair cost sheets.

Note: Where clock cards are used in addition to workshop time sheets the total hours shown on each document should be reconciled weekly.

9.5.2 WORKSHOP PARTS REQUISITION

Parts issued from a firm's own store for repair work are recorded on a workshop parts requisition (*see* Figure 13). A separate requisition is used

WORKSHOP PARTS REQUISITION					
DATE...........		SERIAL No...............			
VEHICLE No..........		JOB No...............			
Part No.	Description	Quantity	Price per unit	£	p
Parts issued by.............		Received by..............			

FIGURE 13. Workshop parts requisition.

for each issue and for each vehicle. The parts used are extended at *cost* price, i.e. the price paid (ignoring cash but including *trade* discount). At the close of each week the workshop parts requisitions are costed and analysed by vehicles, and the costs transferred to the respective vehicle repair cost sheets.

Tyre requisitions

Tyre replacements are issued from stock on a workshop parts requisition in the normal way. The cost, however, is not charged on the vehicle repair cost sheet but is shown at the foot of this form for memorandum purposes only. This is because tyre costs are ultimately shown under tyres on the vehicle cost sheet and not under repairs and maintenance, for the reasons given in Chapter 6 (Section 6.2.3). But where tyres are treated as part of capital cost (i.e. in the depreciation rate) they would of course be charged out on the vehicle cost sheet when replaced.

9.5.3 PARTS STOCK RECONCILIATION

It is not always possible to count stock at the close of each accounting period, especially where large stocks are carried and there is limited experienced staff available for this purpose. Even so a physical stock count should be made at least four times a year if parts and materials are to be rigidly controlled.

Parts and materials should be recorded on bin cards (or a similar record) which give basic information such as: part (or material) name or code number, date (received/issued), name of supplier, number on parts requisi-

STOCK COUNT SHEET AS AT _ _ _ _ _ _ _ _ _ _ _ _ _							
Stock item	Recorded stock	Actual stock	Quantity difference		Unit price	Under £	Over £
			Under	Over			

Counted by _ _ _ _ _ _ _ _ _ _ _ _   Spot-checked by _ _ _ _ _ _ _ _ _ _ _ _ _   Depot _ _ _ _ _ _ _ _ _ _

FIGURE 14. Stock count sheet.

tion (for control purposes), quantity (received, issued, balance), and unit price.

The reputed stock balance at any time is the total of the quantities on hand at the respective cost prices. This should be verified by taking a physical stock count, which entails a systematic count of all stock items after all paperwork (receipts/issues/transfers) up to the date of the stock count has been processed on the stock records. During the stock count there must not be any stock movement either in or out, which is why it is normally undertaken during a weekend.

A stock count sheet is prepared in advance of the stock count as in Figure 14. As each bin or stock is counted, a paper sticker or label is left with the stock showing the quantity counted. (The term 'count' is used broadly and includes count, measure, weigh, etc.) Once the count is complete and the

VEHICLE REPAIR COST SHEET						
VEHICLE No._____ MONTH ENDING_____						
	W/E____ £	W/E____ £	W/E____ £	W/E____ £	W/E____ £	Total £
Labour and overheads						
Parts ex store						
Outside repairs						
Oils and lubricants						
Sundries						
Sub-total						
less paid insurance claims						
Total						
Summary of work done						
Tyres fitted (No. x price)						

FIGURE 15. Vehicle repair cost sheet.

necessary spot checks have been made (i.e. certain stocks are recounted to test the accuracy of the count), the actual quantities are recorded on the stock count sheet and the differences calculated.

Large differences, particularly of an expensive item, would require immediate investigation even though the horse may have bolted. Saleable items such as tyres, batteries, lamps, tools, etc., are the ones where control is most needed; and in a large firm a good, honest storeman – or foreman in the case of a small firm – is an investment in itself. Stock deficits are written off in the financial accounts.

9.5.4 VEHICLE REPAIR COST SHEET

The weekly costs of labour, overheads, and materials are written on the vehicle repair cost sheet and totalled for the month (or four week period) (*see* Figure 15). "Outside" repairs are taken from subcontractors' invoices and analysed over vehicles. The total repair and maintenance costs for each vehicle are transferred to the respective cost sheet.

9.6 VEHICLE COST SHEET

This is the most important form in the costing system because it shows to what extent each vehicle has contributed to the profits of the business. It shows all historical costs and the revenue earned during the accounting period, the difference between the two being a profit or a loss. Specimen vehicle cost sheets are shown in Figures 16 and 17.

9.6.1 COMPILING THE VEHICLE COST SHEET

It will have been gathered from the foregoing that road transport costing is nothing more than simple recording followed by a few simple calculations, e.g. hours × cost rate, litres × unit price. Filling out the form is simplicity itself as by this stage the real work has been done. The process is as described below.

(a) Fixed Costs including Overheads

As already explained, these costs are *annual* costs and are readily obtainable from their various sources (Chapter 6). Once the cost figure for each vehicle has been determined it is a relatively simple task to divide the fixed costs by the number of accounting periods (e.g. thirteen four-week periods or twelve calendar month periods) to arrive at a vehicle fixed cost per accounting period. This is a once-a-year operation involving very little

		Month £	To date £	Unit costs Month £	Unit costs To date £
FIXED COSTS					
	Licence				
	Insurance				
	Depreciation				
	Rent and rates				
	Operating licence				
	Overheads (fleet and admin.)				
DRIVER'S COSTS					
	Wages				
	Expenses				
VARIABLE COSTS					
	Fuel				
	Oil				
	Tyres				
	Repairs and maintenance:				
	Materials				
	Labour				
	Overheads				
	Outside repairs				
TOTAL COSTS					
REVENUE					
PROFIT/(LOSS)					
	Kilometres run				
	Tonnes carried				
	Drops made				

VEHICLE COST SHEET

VEHICLE No. _____

REG. No. _____

DEPOT No. _____

MONTH ENDING _____

Note: 'Unit costs' can be for kilometres run, tonnes carried, tonne-kilometres, litres, packs, etc., depending on the requirements of a business.

FIGURE 16. Vehicle cost sheet (1).

VEHICLE COST SHEET

VEHICLE No. --------------   MONTH ENDING --------------

	km run	Tonnes carried	Drops made	VARIABLE COSTS										Wages and expenses £	Vehicle fixed costs £	Total operating costs £	Revenue £	Gross profit £	Bus. o'head £	Net profit £
				Fuel £	Oil £	Tyres (x c.p.k.*) £	REPAIRS AND MAINTENANCE				Total £	Total variable costs £							
							Lab. and o'head £	Parts £	Outside repairs £	less credits £									
W/E -------																			
W/E -------																			
W/E -------																			
W/E -------																			
W/E -------																			
TOTAL																			
TOTAL TO DATE																			
UNIT COST:																			
MONTH																			
TO DATE																			

(*Cost per km)

Note: This layout enables operating figures to be completed on a weekly basis.

FIGURE 17. Vehicle cost sheet (2).

work other than the compilation of a vehicle fixed-cost schedule for reference purposes.

Although individual fixed costs are shown on the vehicle cost sheet, in fact they could be aggregated, one calculation made, and only the *total* cost figure shown. The figures for the current month are written in the MONTH column on the vehicle cost sheet (or four week-column if such is the case) and *added* to the TO DATE figures for the previous month; the totals are then written in the TO DATE column for the current month.

Example: (Year commencing 1 January)

January		February		March	
MONTH	TO DATE	MONTH	TO DATE	MONTH	TO DATE
410	410	425	835	390	1,225

(b) Wages and expenses

As already stated, wages and expenses, once analysed weekly, are shown on the vehicle record sheet, totalled for the accounting period, and written in the MONTH column on the vehicle cost sheet. The TO DATE figure is obtained by simply adding the current month's figure to the TO DATE figure for the previous month.

Note: When a month end occurs during the week the wages clerk will have to split the payroll accordingly.

(c) Fuel and Oil

Fuel and oil figures have already been shown on the vehicle record sheet. It is therefore a matter of copying the figures on to the vehicle cost sheet. The TO DATE figures on the vehicle cost sheet are obtained as already described.

(d) Tyres

The cost is obtained by taking the kilometres run during the accounting period at the cost rate, and adjusting where necessary for blow outs (but *see also* section 9.5.2).

(e) Repairs and maintenance

The cost is a straight copy from the vehicle repair cost sheet.

(f) Total cost

This is the sum total of all recorded costs in the MONTH and TO DATE columns on the vehicle cost sheet.

(g) *Revenue*

The revenue earned by each vehicle during the accounting period is obtained from the *sales invoice analysis*. Sales invoices are analysed by vehicles on a weekly basis and the total for each vehicle is shown on the respective vehicle record sheet. At period end a grand total is obtained and transferred to the individual vehicle cost sheet.

Note: All sales for the accounting period should be included irrespective of the dates shown on the invoices.

(h) *Profit/(Loss)*

The difference between total cost and revenue will either be a profit or a loss.

(i) *Kilometres run, tonnes carried, drops made*

These are obtained from the vehicle record sheet.

(j) *Unit Costs*

These are MONTH and TO DATE costs on the vehicle cost sheet divided by units which can be either per kilometre, per tonne, or per tonne kilometre, depending on the particular one selected. Other units could be: per cubic metre, per litre, per pack, etc. As the logical cost unit for vehicle variable costs is the kilometre, the same unit could be extended to fixed costs and revenue in order to obtain the profit or loss per kilometre run.

The object of ascertaining unit costs for both MONTH and TO DATE figures is to compare:

1 One month with the average to date, which will ensure that adverse trends are spotted.
2 Similar types of vehicles, e.g. if it were found that one vehicle's variable costs were high when compared with those of an identical vehicle, this would call for investigation.

9.7 FLEET COST-AND-PROFIT STATEMENT

Once the operating profit or loss for each vehicle over the accounting period has been determined, the next logical step is to compile an overall cost-and-profit statement for the entire fleet of vehicles (*see* Figure 18). This may not be so important in a firm employing a small number of vehicles, as the individual vehicle cost sheets would speak for themselves. In large firms where directors and managers have very little time to study

FLEET COST-AND-PROFIT STATEMENT

DEPOT No._____

MONTH ENDING _____

VEHICLE NUMBER	MONTH						TO DATE						MONTH	TO DATE	TO DATE
	Fixed costs * £	Wages and expenses £	Variable costs £	Total costs £	Revenue £	Profit/(Loss) £	Fixed costs * £	Wages and expenses £	Variable costs £	Total costs £	Revenue £	Profit/(Loss) £	Profit/(Loss) per unit £	Profit/(Loss) per unit £	% Profit of Total

(* Including business overhead)

FIGURE 18. Fleet cost-and-profit statement.

each vehicle's performance in detail, an overall profit-and-loss statement would show at a glance:

1 The overall profit or loss for the accounting period.
2 The extent to which each vehicle has contributed to the overall result.

Where a manager is dissatisfied and requires more detail of a particular vehicle (or group of vehicles) it is simply a matter of referring to the vehicle cost sheet(s) in question. An ideal situation would be to present the directors and managers at each accounting-period end with a fleet cost-and-profit statement with copies of the vehicle cost sheets attached.

The compilation of the statement is simplicity itself as the figures are copied direct from the individual vehicle cost sheets, the only complication being that it is first necessary to total the fixed and variable costs on each vehicle cost sheet before entering on the cost-and-profit statement. This forms an independent check on the arithmetical accuracy of the vehicle cost sheets.

9.7.1 INTERPRETATION OF FLEET COST-AND-PROFIT STATEMENT

It should be remembered that a costing system is designed to aid management by goading it into action where the demand justifies, and by helping management make decisions when the need arises. Unlike the annual accounts of a limited company where everything has to be correct to the nearest penny, costing is less precise as figures have to be produced promptly if management is to take any necessary corrective action. When reading cost-and-profit data the following points should be borne in mind:

1 *Costing data is not 100% correct*, for the reasons given below. Most of the figures are based on known facts at the time, however, and are therefore reliable for management purposes, which is their sole objective.
2 *Overheads and prices may have changed*, in which case current figures should be adjusted accordingly. In the case of overheads, however, items such as stationery, lighting, telephones, etc. can never be accurately estimated and the level of actual overheads should be constantly watched.
3 *Repairs and maintenance costs should be looked at over a period rather than monthly*, as a healthy vehicle profit shown one month could easily be absorbed by a heavy repair bill during the following month.
4 *Stock losses such as fuel and parts are seldom included on the cost-and-profit statement*, although there is no reason why they should not be included.

The cost-and-profit statement is therefore a valuable management guide so long as it is remembered that it has its limitations.

9.8 SUMMARY

Figure 19 shows the flow of information and documentation.

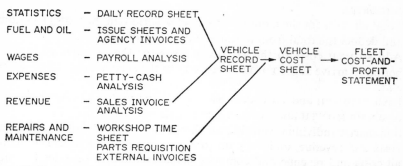

Note: Weekly repairs and maintenance figures could be shown instead on the vehicle record sheet and transferred to the vehicle cost sheet with the other costs. Tyre costs are calculated on the vehicle cost sheet unless treated as a capital cost.

FIGURE 19. Cost flow analysis.

9.8.1 WEEKLY

1 Obtain individual vehicle statistics (kilometres, tonnes, drops, etc.) from *daily record sheets* and show on *vehicle record sheets.*

2 Obtain fuel and oil issues to vehicles from *fuel and oil issue sheets* and show on individual *vehicle record sheets.*

3 Obtain agency invoices for fuel and oil supplied on the road, analyse by vehicles, and summarize on *vehicle record sheets.*

4 Obtain *workshop time sheets* and *workshop parts requisitions* from workshop foreman (or cost office) and summarize on *vehicle repair cost sheet.*

5 Obtain 'outside' invoices for repairs and maintenance, summarize by vehicles, and show on *vehicle repair cost sheet.*

6 Obtain 'drivers'' wages and expenses and show on *vehicle record sheet.*

7 Obtain *sales invoice analysis* and show individual vehicle revenue on *vehicle record sheet.*

9.8.2 MONTHLY (OR FOUR-WEEKLY)

1 Total figures on *vehicle record sheets* and post to individual *vehicle cost sheets.*

2 Total figures on *vehicle repair cost sheet* and post to individual *vehicle cost sheets.*

3 Extend tyres cost in tyre column by taking the total kilometres run at the appropriate tyre cost rate (unless tyres are treated as capital, in which case show new-tyre costs only).

4 Obtain from fixed-costs schedule (or previous *vehicle cost sheet*) the various fixed costs including overheads and show on individual *vehicle cost sheets.*

5 Total all costs for the month (or four-week period) in the MONTH column and deduct the total from revenue to obtain profit or loss.

6 Add MONTH costs to the TO DATE costs for the previous accounting period to arrive at the TO DATE costs up to the current accounting-period end.

7 Divide MONTH and TO DATE costs by selected unit (e.g. kilometres run) to obtain MONTH and TO DATE unit costs.

8 Summarize individual vehicle cost sheets into fixed, variable, and wages costs and revenue, and copy on to *fleet cost-and-profit statement.* Total all costs and revenue and complete percentage return on sales for each vehicle.

9 Study cost data and take immediate action where necessary.

10 Rate Fixing and Profit

It was stated in Chapter 4 that costing and estimating are quite separate functions, although basic costing information is – and should be – used in estimating. Costing is concerned with what has actually been spent or incurred, i.e. is done *after* an event has taken place, while estimating or rate fixing is concerned with pricing some future job or contract. Costing tells us how much profit was made or what loss was sustained and therefore how accurate (or inaccurate) an estimate was – from which it can be deduced that costing is an easier science than estimating.

10.1 PRICING POLICY

Every business should have a pricing policy, even if it is the common practice of charging something less than the local rate for a job. If an operator is sensible, however, he will formulate his own price structure after first deciding the prices he ought to be charging having regard to the business risk involved and the capital employed in the business. To say that a pricing policy is impossible in road transport operations because of local rates and competition, is really begging the question. The time is coming when every operator will have to stand on his own two feet; with rising costs and increasing legislation many firms are falling by the wayside, small firms in particular. In fact the existing number of road haulage firms is expected to drop over the next few years as the result of liquidations, takeovers, and mergers. This does not mean that competition will diminish; if anything it will increase, though on a more scientific scale. The road haulage industry is now aware that the cut-throat attitude of the past (i.e. rate cutting) is no longer viable if long-term success is to be the goal. There will still be price cutting in the sense that jobs will go to the operator who can offer the best service at the lowest price; but the operator will first ensure that his 'lowest price' is sufficient to generate adequate profit. In other words, operators should seek to maintain satisfactory price levels from which the industry will gain, rather than reduce them to give-away prices.

10.2 KNOW YOUR COSTS

The first thing an operator should learn about rate fixing is the importance of *knowing* his costs. Unless an operator knows how much it costs to run his vehicles, including business overheads, there is very little chance of his establishing realistic traffic rates for each of his vehicles.

To begin with, all costs should be separated into *fixed* and *variable* costs following normal costing practice. The costs are then adjusted to allow for known or expected increases including the replacement price of a vehicle. Repair and maintenance costs present a problem in that they are not always determinable, in which case a sensible estimate must be made.

Example:

The following details have been taken from a firm's cost records:

Vehicle XYZ: 20-tonne payload

Annual fixed costs	(£)	Variable costs per kilometre (pence)	
Licences	420	Fuel and oil	5·0
Insurance	360	Tyres	1·5
Depreciation	1,000	Repairs and maintenance	1·7
Overheads	800		
Wages	850		

Notes:

1 The cost of the vehicle (bought four years ago) was £6,000 (without tyres). The replacement price today is £7,200.
2 Tyres are treated as a running cost, not capitalized with the vehicle.
3 Fuel, oil, and tyres are expected to increase shortly by 5 per cent.
4 The commercial life of the vehicle is reckoned at six years.
5 The insurance premium is expected to increase by 10 per cent and overheads by 5 per cent.
6 The annual activity is approximately 40,000 km.
7 The workshop foreman reckons that the vehicle's maintenance costs over the year will work out at about £800.

The costs are therefore adjusted as follows:

Annual fixed costs	Original	Revised
Licences	420	420
Insurance	360	396
Depreciation	1,000	1,200
Overheads	800	840
Wages	850	850
	3,430	3,706

Variable costs per kilometre (pence)		
Fuel and oil	5·0	5·3
Tyres	1·5	1·6
Repairs and maintenance	1·7	2·0
	8·2	8·9

The operator now knows what his costs should be for the ensuing trading year. He also knows that they have to be recovered in the rates charged for vehicle operations before he can hope to make a profit. He is particularly concerned with the annual fixed costs because, even if traffic falls off, these costs will remain.

The next step is to determine the profit factor.

10.3 HOW MUCH PROFIT?

A business must aim for the economic profit required for its maintenance and development. Long-term success should be the aim rather than short-term profit. How is the profit objective determined? By many operators it is determined on a cost-plus basis, i.e. estimated cost *plus x* per cent for profit. Although operators may get by using this method it is never really satisfactory unless it is related to the capital employed in a business. It could in fact be part of the reason why the return on capital employed is so low in the road haulage industry. The method also precludes the element of risk.

10.3.1 CAPITAL EMPLOYED AND RISK FACTORS

By definition, capital employed is the sum of issued share capital, reserves, and long-term loans. Put another way, it is total assets *less* current liabilities. The following simplified balance sheet illustrates this clearly.

Example:

The Trucking Co. Ltd
Balance Sheet as at 19...

	£		£
Issued share capital	40,000	Fixed assets	50,000
Profit & loss account	5,000		
12% debentures	10,000		
	55,000		
Current liabilities	5,000	Current assets	10,000
	60,000		60,000

(Capital employed = total assets (£60,000) *less* current liabilities (£5,000) = £55,000.)

It can be seen that the capital employed in the business is £55,000, made up of: £40,000 provided by the shareholders, who are the rightful owners; £5,000, which is the favourable balance on the profit-and-loss account (i.e. the cumulative net profit earned to date and carried forward after dividends and taxation); and £10,000 provided by the debenture holder(s), which is a loan for a fixed number of years. In each case the money is deployed in the business to finance the purchase of premises, vehicles, plant, and other fixed assets, and as working capital to cover fuel, oil, parts, wages, and other operating expenses. This, then, is the capital employed in the business from which profit must be earned to:

1 Pay an annual dividend to the shareholders.
2 Pay debenture interest (whether a profit is made or not).
3 Generate sufficient surplus to finance the growing needs of the business in terms of fixed and working capital.

10.3.2 RETURN ON CAPITAL

The question remains: How much profit? The concept of capital employed is that money invested in a business should earn a return at least equal to what it would earn if invested in the money market. For instance, if capital of £55,000 was invested on the stock exchange it might earn a return of about 9 per cent. Should, then, an operator's profit objective be the same, i.e. 9 per cent on capital employed? The answer is that it should be much higher – because of the element of risk in running a business. Moreover, if the current money market rate was the aim it would pay an operator to sell out, invest his money, play golf all day, and so forgo all the work and worry connected with running a business. The fact of the matter is that an operator is in business to make a good deal more than the current market rate of return on capital, which involves a risk, as many operators know too well. The return on capital should therefore be at least 20 per cent before taxation, and even this may be too low in a world where prices are steadily rising and the value of money falling.

10.3.3 CALCULATING PROFIT

Calculating the profit to be earned on capital employed presents no problem. Taking the above balance sheet the calculation is simply:

$$£55,000 \times 20/100 = £11,000$$

The sum of £11,000 is the desired net profit before taxation for the business as a whole and must therefore be reflected in the traffic rates. How is this done?

10.4 DETERMINING TRAFFIC RATES

10.4.1 PROFIT LOADING

In regard to the imaginary company in Chapter 7 (section 7.2.3) it was recommended that overheads should be apportioned on the basis of payload when payloads vary from vehicle to vehicle. The reason given was that it is wrong to burden a 7-tonne vehicle with the same overheads as a 20-tonne vehicle, as such practice could easily lead to loss of orders. The same reasoning is applied to profit loading: each vehicle should carry its fair share of profit according to its revenue-earning capacity. So it would be wrong to expect a 7-tonne vehicle to earn the same amount of profit as a 20-tonne vehicle, assuming the same volume of activity in each case.

For the imaginary fleet of twelve vehicles the annual profit loadings would be as follows:

$$£11,000 \div 143 \text{ tonnes} = £76 \cdot 923 \text{ per tonne payload}$$

$$
\begin{array}{llll}
\text{20-tonne vehicles:} & 20 \times £76\cdot923 &= £1,538 \\
15 \quad ,, \quad\quad ,, & 15 \times £76\cdot923 &= £1,154 \\
10 \quad ,, \quad\quad ,, & 10 \times £76\cdot923 &= £769 \\
7 \quad ,, \quad\quad ,, & 7 \times £76\cdot923 &= £538 \\
\end{array}
$$

Proof of calculation:

	Profit loading £
2 vehicles, 20 tonnes each (2 × £1,538)	3,076
3 ,, 15 ,, ,, (3 × £1,154)	3,462
3 ,, 10 ,, ,, (3 × £769)	2,307
4 ,, 7 ,, ,, (4 × £538)	2,152
	10,997

(*Note:* the difference of £3 is due to rounding.)

10.4.2 TIME AND DISTANCE FACTORS

Once the desired profit per vehicle per annum has been calculated it must be decided whether the profit should be loaded on the basis of time, kilometres or both. If it is loaded on a time basis it is simply a matter of adding the profit to the annual fixed costs. For the 20-tonne XYZ vehicle the sum would be:

Annual fixed costs	£3,706
Annual profit loading	£1,538
	£5,244

If it is loaded on the basis of estimated annual kilometres run (e.g. 40,000 km) the sum would be:

Variable costs per kilometre	8·90p
Profit loading per kilometre	3·84p*
	12·74p

(*£1,538 ÷ 40,000)

There is an opinion that profit loading should be on a time basis, the argument being that profit should be made *daily* irrespective of the number of

A/658.91

kilometres involved. The argument against this is that long-distance runs tend to be subsidized at the expense of short runs, i.e. it costs a customer no more to have a load delivered 70 km away than to have it delivered 50 km away. But where time is the key factor rather than distance there is a case for the time basis.

For the average haulier who is involved in a variety of long- and short-distance work it is preferable to load profit on both time and distance. If, for example, our XYZ vehicle was employed on long-, medium- and short-distance work, one half of the profit could be loaded on time and the other half on kilometres, as follows:

Annual fixed costs	£3,706
Annual profit loading ($\frac{1}{2}$)	£769
	£4,475

Variable costs per kilometre	8·90p
Profit loading per kilometre ($\frac{1}{2}$)	1·92p
	10.82p

When the time/distance ratio is known by vehicles, profit should be loaded in the same ratio.

10.4.3 VEHICLE UTILIZATION

Annual fixed or time costs should be recovered on a time basis; so once the annual fixed cost has been ascertained the next step is to calculate the actual number of operating days in a trading year. This figure is obtained by taking the total number of working days in a year and deducting from it the number of anticipated idle days.

Example:

XYZ Vehicle

	Days	
52 × 5$\frac{1}{2}$-day week	286	
less Holiday shut-down including bank holidays ⎫ Maintenance and testing ⎭	(42)	
Operating days available	242	(84%)

The off-road time shown in the example is purely imaginary and in practice would be obtained by estimating very carefully the number of days involved for each item. If the 242 days is correct this would be the number of days during which the vehicle would operate to earn the planned profit of £1,538. The need for accuracy cannot be overemphasized, e.g. if only 235 days were worked there would be a loss of income resulting from unrecovered overheads and lost profit.

10.4.4 ESTABLISHING A VEHICLE RATE

With the above information available a vehicle rate can now be established:

1 *Rate per day:*
   £4,475 ÷ 242 = £18·492 (say £18·50) *plus*
2 *Rate per kilometre* 10·82p.

Instead of using the rate per day a rate per hour could be calculated by reducing the total number of operating days to hours.

10.4.5 THE 'TOTAL RATE PER KILOMETRE' FALLACY

Some hauliers favour a total rate per kilometre. In the above case the rate would be derived as follows:

Fixed rate per kilometre	11·18p*
Variable rate per kilometre	10·82p
	22·00p

(*£4,475 ÷ 40,000)

As the rate is based on estimated annual kilometres it may be assumed to be reasonable. In practice, however, it does not always work out.

Example:

Suppose a haulier has to quote for a job involving a total distance of 100 km, there and back. Assume the trip is through a densely populated area and will take a whole day. Using the total rate per kilometre (ignoring competition) the quotation would be:

   100 km at 22·00p per km = £22·00

No doubt the rate would be accepted. If we look at our time and kilometre rate, however, we see that the fixed rate per day would be £18·50 alone! Bringing in the variable cost per kilometre the quotation should really be:

Fixed rate per day	£18·50
Variable rate: 100 km at 10·82p	£10·82
	£29·32
plus Driver's expenses (if any)	

Clearly something is wrong somewhere in spite of the costs having been carefully compiled and the profit carefully computed.

The answer lies, of course, in the time costs. The cost per day is right and cannot be faulted. Only when it is related to kilometres does it go wrong. The fact of the matter is that, to recover £18·50 on a kilometre basis the vehicle must cover 165 km *per day* (i.e. 40,000 km ÷ 242 days). If it does less than this distance the full daily rate will not be recovered. It is therefore up to every haulier who uses this method of pricing to first ensure that the 'fixed daily kilometres' are capable of attainment. If they are not then the traditional method (time and kilometres) should be used.

A way around the problem is to establish a total cost-and-profit rate per kilometre per day, so that whatever kilometres are run per day the same level of profit (the planned profit) will be earned. This is illustrated in Figure 21.

10.4.6 DRIVER'S WAGES AND EXPENSES

In the example in section 10.4.5 driver's wages were included with annual fixed costs while expenses were added separately. There is an argument for treating both wages and expenses as a separate entity when quoting prices, due to factors such as overtime, overnight stops, tolls, and other expenses On the other hand, basic wages could be included under annual fixed costs with overtime pay, overnight allowance, and other expenses added to the quotation. The latter is considered preferable.

10.5 RATES SCHEDULE

Rates should be computed for each vehicle (or group of similar vehicles in the case of a large company) in the manner described above, and a rates schedule compiled from them. Some rates schedules are shown in Figures 20 and 21 as a guide.

10.5.1 INTERPRETATION OF RATES SCHEDULE

Having compiled a rates schedule an operator can see at a glance what his operating costs are and what profit he intends to make from each vehicle. If competition did not exist the schedule could be used without problem. Competition does exist, however, and the schedule has to be used in a sensible flexible way. In other words, the rates shown in the schedule should not be regarded as so *fixed* that work is lost through rigid adherence to the schedule. In practice an operator would seek to obtain the highest price possible for carrying a load or the minimum price to secure an order. *But with the rates schedule by his side he will know exactly how far he*

	Vehicle 1	Vehicle 2	Vehicle 3	Vehicle 4	Vehicle 5	Vehicle 6	Vehicle 7	Vehicle 8	Vehicle 9
	£	£	£	£	£	£	£	£	£
ANNUAL FIXED: Licences Insurance Depreciation Garaging Overhead Basic wages									
TOTAL									
	p	p	p	p	p	p	p	p	p
VARIABLE COSTS PER km: Fuel and oil Tyres Maintenance									
TOTAL									
TOTAL FIXED PROFIT LOADING									
TOTAL									
OPERATING DAYS TOTAL VARIABLE PROFIT LOADING									
TOTAL PER km									
ANNUAL km									
FIXED RATE PER DAY									
FIXED RATE PER HOUR									
VARIABLE RATE PER km									

ABC HAULAGE CO. LTD

BASIC RATES SCHEDULE — EFFECTIVE FROM _____

Note: Rates should be increased for overtime premium, overnight allowances, tolls, etc., as the case may be.

FIGURE 20. Rates schedule (1).

FIXED COSTS AND PROFIT PER WEEKLY KILOMETRES					
Based on 46 working weeks	8 tonne	10 tonne	13 tonne	15 tonne	20 tonne
PER WEEK			£41.85 or 4 185p		
km PER WEEK* 200			p 20.92		
300			13.95		
400			10.46		
500			8.37		
600			6.97		
700			5.98		
800			5.23		
900			4.65		
1 000			4.18		
1 100			3.80		
1 200			3.49		
1 300			3.22		
1 400			2.99		
plus Variable costs and profit			5.89		
Driver's wages, nat. ins. and grad. pension, holiday pay, subsistence money, profit margin to be added (per km)					
CHARGE PER km					

(*Alternatively a cost-and-profit rate per km-day could be drawn up)

FIGURE 21. Rates schedule (2).

can go with rate manipulation, i.e. whether he is making a profit or merely breaking even on a job or contract.

A short study of the rates schedule calculated in section 10.4 incorporating our XYZ vehicle, would bring these points home to an operator:

1 To achieve profit target a fixed charge of £18·50 per day must be made for 242 days of the year, and a variable charge of 10·82p per km must be made for 40,000 km during the year.
2 Rates higher than £18·50 per day and 10·82p per km will enhance profit, while lower rates will reduce profit.
3 If more than 242 days can be worked during the year or more than 40,000 km covered at the scheduled rates, profit will be enhanced; the reverse will diminish profit.
4 To break even (i.e. the vehicle makes neither a profit nor a loss) charges must not fall below £15·32 per day (£3,706 ÷ 242 days) nor below 8·90p per km over the operating year.
5 In cases of severe competition the operator can see that any price received in excess of 8·90p per km would contribute towards the vehicle's fixed costs of £3,706. This is the marginal-cost or contribution approach (discussed in Chapter 13).

An operator armed with this knowledge and a regular cost-reporting system is in a far better position to control his business than the average operator who poaches his fellow operators' rates and does not employ a costing system.

10.5.2 PUBLISHED RATES

Annual guide rates are published by the *Commercial Motor* and *Motor Transport* with a view to helping operators with their own rate fixing. Although this is to be commended there is no substitute for establishing one's own rates schedule, as overheads vary from business to business; and the operator who has the long-term success of his business at heart will attempt to do this.

10.6 RENTING OUT TRACTORS AND TRAILERS

Where tractors and trailers are rented out for profit the procedure to adopt is the same as that already described, namely:

1 Establish time and running costs where rates are based on these factors, i.e. £x per day plus a rate per kilometre run.

2 Adjust costs where necessary for excessive wear and tear due to nature of loads carried, terrain, etc.

3 Add profit figure.

Bear in mind that most hirers usually provide their own fuel and oil, while the cost of repairs and maintenance, tyres, etc., will be borne by the hire company. Adjustment must therefore be made for these items in the hire rate. Also bear in mind that trailers are better charged out on a rate-per-day basis, running costs such as tyres and maintenance being covered within the rate. When drivers are provided by the company then either a separate rate can be charged (some hirers prefer this) or their cost may be included in the daily hire rate.

Where renting-out is a major activity it is as well to treat it as a separate trading division. This means that all costs and expenses associated with the division will be charged to it. In other words, the division will have its own fleet of tractors and/or trailers, incur its own office expenses, plus maybe a 'management charge', and possibly have its own workshop facilities. Alternatively in the latter case, charges for repairs and maintenance could be made to the division by the central workshop which, as we saw in Chapter 8, is a separate cost centre.

10.7 SUMMARY

1 A pricing (rate-fixing) policy is an important feature of road haulage operations. Long-term business success should be the goal rather than a quick but short profit.

2 It is impossible to compile a realistic rates schedule unless all business costs are known and identified. Basic costs should be revised where changes are expected.

3 Profit goals should be based on the capital employed and risk factors rather than on just a profit uplift on costs.

4 Where vehicles are dissimilar profit loading should be based on payload.

5 Rates should normally be charged on a time and distance basis having regard to the anticipated kilometres per annum (or shorter period) and operating days (i.e. expected utilization).

6 The 'total rate per km' method of charging for work can be dangerous where the actual daily kilometres are less than the anticipated daily kilometres (i.e. total annual kilometres divided by net operating days).

7 Wages are sometimes treated as a separate charge rather than as part of the daily rate.

8 Where a business hires out tractors, trailers, and drivers on a regular basis the activity should be treated as a separate trading division for profit-and-loss accounting purposes.

Part Three

FINANCIAL PLANNING AND CONTROL

11 Budgetary Control

In Part Two the recording and analysis of historical data for information purposes were discussed. To be worthwhile, however, the operating information produced should be related to what *should* be happening in the business. No manager worth his salt would be prepared to sit back and let a business follow its own course. Part Three therefore turns to the important subject of business planning, though mainly from the financial point of view. It starts with short-term financial planning (budgets, standard costs, etc.) and ends by taking a look at the more important long-range business planning.

11.1 PLANNING AND BUDGETING

11.1.1 THE NEED FOR PLANNING

Some people have odd views about budgets. Quite a few believe that a budget is based on what happened during the previous year, in terms of income and expenditure, plus an uplift (e.g. 5–10 per cent) to allow for increased costs. Nothing could be further from the truth, yet many companies operate this 'method' and wonder why it proves to be a meaningless exercise.

Budgeting begins with *planning*; in fact it is nothing more than the evaluation in monetary and quantitative terms of a business plan. Some of the basic considerations which precede planning are:

1 The capital invested in the business.
2 The desired rate of return on capital employed.
3 Whether the desired rate will be achieved if the company continues to operate in its present form.
4 If the answer to (3) is in the negative, the steps that need to be taken to bridge the profit gap. This may necessitate consideration of the following:
   (*a*) The required level of sales during the plan period.
   (*b*) The rates to be charged.
   (*c*) The allowed cost of sales (i.e. fleet operating costs).
   (*d*) The allowed level of overhead expenditure.
   (*e*) The resources needed to achieve the desired sales level (e.g. number

E

and types of vehicles, workshop equipment, personnel and administrative facilities, working capital, etc.).

5 After the steps to be taken to bridge the profit gap have been decided, the control information required to show whether or not the profit plan is being achieved.

6 The plan time-scale and the number of accounting (or control) periods per trading year, e.g. twelve calendar months or thirteen four-week periods.

Except for capital-intensive industries the normal practice is to plan for some five years ahead, the first year in detail, the remaining years in outline only. Once the long-term plan (discussed separately in Chapter 17) has been defined and agreed by those responsible for its implementation and achievement, it is quantified in the form of a series of budgets (which sometimes call for *replanning* if the monetary results do not work out as intended); these relate specifically to the first year of the plan.

11.1.2 TYPES OF BUDGETS

Budgets are concerned with income, expenditure, and the employment of capital, because that is what financial planning is all about. In road transport there are at least three budgets which are of interest to managers:

1 The operating budget, principally concerned with sales income, operating costs, and overheads.
2 The capital expenditure budget, principally concerned with expenditure on replacement vehicles, workshop equipment, office furniture and equipment, etc.
3 The cash budget, principally concerned with cash flow and all that it entails.

Together they make up the *master* (or total) budget.

11.1.3 THE BUDGET PERIOD

The time span of the financial plan must be clearly defined. Normally it is geared to a company's yearly trading cycle but will be projected several years hence, the first year in detail and the later years in outline only – i.e. projected sales, costs and profits, capital requirements (e.g. fleet size), etc. Each trading year is broken down into control periods, either calendar months or four-week periods, when actual performance is measured against budgeted performance. Swift action can then be taken when deviations emerge. Although fixed for a period of time (i.e. one year) the budget itself

s by no means fixed but is updated as situations change. It is not uncommon
o review a budget once every quarter and revise it if necessary.

A budget may therefore be defined as a plan expressed in quantitative
ınd monetary terms, relating to a period of time. In practice, planning and
ıudgeting never cease and form an on-going process.

1.2 THREE TYPES OF BUDGETS

1.2.1 OPERATING BUDGETS

The operating budget deals with the daily operations of the business in
erms of the volume of sales, the rates to be charged, and the allowed costs
ınd expenses, which are geared, of course, to the sales volume. It is made up
ıf a number of functional budgets, namely, the sales budget, fleet operating
ıudget, workshop budget, and administration budget.

a) *Sales budget*

As a company's operation is centred on sales activity the first budget to
ompile is the sales budget, based on the sales forecast for each vehicle (or
ıroup of vehicles) for the trading year. Factors to consider are:

Vehicle capacity and utilization (i.e. load potential and shift working).
The volume and types of traffic carried at the various rates.
Possible market changes (i.e. new traffic, the possibility of losing traffic,
new competition, etc.).
Possible policy changes (i.e. the elimination of certain traffic, changing to
different types of vehicles, etc.).

'his kind of analysis would, of course, form part of the planning process,
ınd it is mentioned here to draw the matter to the reader's attention. There
ıay also be many other considerations better known to the reader which
ıeed to be taken into account. To put the matter in a nutshell, it is important
ıat in the final analysis the sales budget is meaningful, based on fact, and
ıpable of attainment under the planned environment. Unless this is so
ɔmparison with actual performance will be meaningless. Where com-
ınies, branches, and depots enjoy a regular flow of traffic from familiar
ıstomers the task is that much easier; this is the one case when the past
ın be of assistance in planning and forecasting.

Once the sales budget has been determined (by extending the vehicle sales
ɔlumes at the various freight rates and arriving at a total for each control
ɛriod) and also the budgeted cost of sales (*see* section (*b*) below), a vehicle
ıles budget and a fleet sales budget can be drawn up (*see* Figures 22 and 23).

VEHICLE SALES BUDGET 19___

VEHICLE: BRANCH/DEPOT:

FLEET No.:

19___	Sales £	Cost of sales £	Budgeted profit £
January			
February			
March			
April			
May			
June			
July			
August			
September			
October			
November			
December			
TOTAL			

Budgeted operating days/hours   --------------------

    ,,   ,,   kilometres   --------------------

    ,,   ,,   units carried   --------------------

Note: 'Units' applies to tonnes, packs, litres, etc., depending on the type of traffic carrie
When the units are mixed, further analysis would be required and the various budgeted uni
stated on the form.

FIGURE 22. Vehicle sales budget.

FLEET SALES BUDGET 19___ BRANCH/DEPOT:			
19___	Sales £	Cost of sales £	Budgeted profit £
January			
February			
March			
April			
May			
June			
July			
August			
September			
October			
November			
December			
TOTAL			
Last year			

FIGURE 23. Fleet sales budget.

Whether the procedure should be approached from the point of view of the total sales budget (based on orders, etc.) being broken down to vehicles (or groups of vehicles), or being built up from individual vehicles, depends on the type and size of business.

(b) Fleet operating budget

Where standard costing is employed (discussed in the following chapter) the task of preparing a fleet operating budget becomes fairly straightforward. In most cases it is simply a matter of extending the time and distance factors at the appropriate standard costs. The budgeted costs should be shown on the vehicle sales and fleet sales budget statements as in Figures 22 and 23. Note that the illustrations are for guideline purposes only; in practice it is necessary to support each monthly set of figures with the factors involved i.e. time, distance, costs, and rates. (*See* Figure 24.)

(c) Workshop budget

The preparation of the workshop operating budget differs from the technique described in Chapter 8 only in that it should be geared to the planned fleet activity. It stands to reason that the higher the fleet activity the higher will be the demand for service and repairs, and therefore the higher will be the operating costs.

(d) Administration budget

The administration budget is made up of management, administration and office expenses which are subdivided into various control (or budget) centres such as management, traffic office, accounts office, and so on. Each expense is studied individually and related to staff and office requirements and budgeted activity (i.e. sales and therefore fleet operations). An example of an administration budget is shown in Figure 25. The budget is built up on a time basis (i.e. weekly or monthly) and culminates in an annual budget, but control is exercised through the calendar month or four-week budget.

11.2.2 CAPITAL EXPENDITURE BUDGET

This budget summarizes the expenditure on fixed assets during the budget period and includes vehicles, office furniture and equipment, staff cars, workshop equipment, etc. It is based on the following information:

1 The budgeted sales activity (and therefore the vehicles and other assets required to meet the sales budget).
2 The age and condition of existing vehicles and plant.

FLEET OPERATING BUDGET — YEAR ENDING _____					
Expenses	Total £	First quarter £	Second quarter £	Third quarter £	Fourth quarter £
Wages and payroll costs					
Vehicle fixed					
Fuel and oil					
Tarpaulins, tyres, flaps, and tubes					
Sheets and ropes					
External repairs					
Workshop					
Other costs (including fleet spares)					
TOTAL					
Budgeted km					
'' tonnes					
'' drops					
'' utilization	%	%	%	%	%

FIGURE 24. Fleet operating budget.

ADMINISTRATION BUDGET – YEAR ENDING_____					
Expenses	Management £	Traffic £	Accounts £	Insurance £	General £
Directors' fees					
Salaries and wages					
Related payroll costs					
Rent and rates					
Light and heat					
Insurance					
Telephone and telex					
Printing and stationery					
Postage					
Subscriptions					
Travelling					
Entertaining					
Cars and expenses					
Legal and professional					
Depreciation					
Repairs and maintenance					
Cleaning					
Training					
Bad debts					
Bank charges					
Advertising					
Welfare					
Other					
TOTAL					
Staff – male					
Staff – female					
Assets employed					

FIGURE 25. Administration budget.

3 Replacement policy.
4 Reports from senior personnel (e.g. depot manager, workshop super-intendent, accountant, etc.) on the need to buy or replace equipment within their control.
5 The long-term business plan.

Whatever the source of information each request should be carefully examined to ascertain whether or not the proposed expenditure is necessary and where it fits into the company's overall business plan. A formal capital expenditure procedure should be set up so that management knows at any point in time the total amount of capital expenditure required, the sum total already committed, the amount expended to date, and the balance outstanding (*see* Figure 26).

11.2.3 CASH BUDGET

The object of the cash budget is to ensure that there is adequate cash available to finance the company's short-term operation as defined in the operating and capital budgets. The need for outside fundings also enters into the cash budget.

There are two ways of preparing a cash budget. The first is the cash flow method; it takes the opening cash balance or deficit, adds cash receipts for the period, and deducts payments, leaving a cash balance or deficit. The timing of receipts and payments is important, as a delay in debtor payments could easily impede operating and capital expenditure. The second method of preparing a cash budget is the balance sheet change method: the budgeted assets and liabilities at the end of each control period are calculated excluding cash, and the difference between the two represents the cash balance or deficit. The first method is outlined in Figure 27 while the second is incorporated with the text in section 11.3 below.

11.3 THE MASTER BUDGET

The master (or total) budget is made up from the individual budgets. It is expressed in the form of a budgeted profit-and-loss statement and a balance sheet for each budget year and each control period. Although the illustration in Figure 28 shows an annual profit statement divided into quarters, the practice should be to have a separate statement for each control period. The same applies to the budgeted balance sheet (or *position* statement) shown in Figure 29.

The example that follows outlines how the budgeted balance sheet is

CAPITAL EXPENDITURE BUDGET – YEAR ENDING ....

	Jan. £	Feb. £	Mar. £	Apr. £	May £	June £	July £	Aug. £	Sep. £	Oct. £	Nov. £	Dec. £
FLEET: (Detail)												
WORKSHOP (Detail)												
ADMINISTRATION (Detail)												

Note: A description of the asset to be purchased would be detailed under each heading (e.g. Fleet) and the amount to be expended (less known allowances, if any) shown in the appropriate control column. The budget should reflect what has been agreed in the overall budget plan and extend into other years.

FIGURE 26. Capital expenditure budget.

CASH BUDGET – YEAR ENDING ----------

		Jan. £	Feb. £	Mar. £	Apr. £	May £	June £	July £	Aug. £	Sep. £	Oct. £	Nov. £	Dec. £
OPENING BALANCE	(1)												
RECEIPTS:													
Trade Debtors													
Cash sales													
Other receipts													
Capital													
TOTAL	(2)												
PAYMENTS:													
Trade creditors													
Hire purchase creditors													
Wages and salaries													
N.H.I. etc.													
Inland revenue													
Other payments													
TOTAL	(3)												
CASH BALANCE/ (1)+(2)–(3) (DEFICIT)													

FIGURE 27. Cash budget.

built up from anticipated balance sheet changes. For illustration purposes the matter has, of course, been simplified, but the principles remain true:

Example:

Balance Sheet as at 31 December 1975

	£	£
Fixed assets		
Vehicles at cost	25,000	
less Depreciation	(11,000)	14,000
Other assets at cost	5,000	
less Depreciation	(2,000)	3,000
		17,000
Current assets		
Stock	3,500	
Debtors	9,500	
Bank	1,000	14,000
		31,000
Share capital		20,000
Profit-and-loss account		2,000
Loan		—
Current liabilities		9,000
		31,000

The budgeted data for the year ending 31 December 1976 is as follows (values only):

1 New vehicles to be bought, costing £10,000, and other fixed assets, costing £1,500.
2 Depreciation charges for year to be: vehicles, £7,000; other assets, £1,000.
3 Stocks to decrease by £500, debtors by £2,500, and current liabilities by £1,000.
4 Net profit (ignoring taxation and dividends) to be budgeted at £1,000 for the year.
5 A medium-term loan of £5,000 to be obtained to support the capital expansion and working-capital position of the business.

The budgeted balance sheet is thus obtained (p. 123) by reflecting the anticipated changes on the last balance sheet, the cash balance being the difference between the budgeted asset and liability figures.

Generally speaking, the cash flow method, as outlined in Figure 27, is used for short-term budgeting (e.g. monthly or quarterly) while the balance sheet change method is normally used for long-term cash budgeting (e.g. three years or more).

	Total £	First quarter £	Second quarter £	Third quarter £	Fourth quarter £
BUDGETED PROFIT STATEMENT – YEAR ENDING_____					
1 SALES					
2 OPERATING COSTS:					
Wages and payroll					
Vehicle fixed					
Tyres, flaps, tubes, etc.					
Sheets and ropes					
External repairs					
Workshop					
Other costs					
TOTAL					
3 GROSS PROFIT (1-2)					
4 ADMINISTRATION					
Management					
Traffic					
Accounts					
Insurance					
General					
TOTAL					
5 MISCELLANEOUS:					
Income					
Expenses					
TOTAL					
6 OPERATING PROFIT (3 - 4 ± 5)					
7 RETURN ON SALES	%	%	%	%	%
8 RETURN ON CAPITAL	%	%	%	%	%

FIGURE 28. Budgeted profit statement.

BUDGETED BALANCE SHEET – YEAR ENDING _____				
	First quarter £	Second quarter £	Third quarter £	Fourth quarter £
FIXED ASSETS (NET):				
Buildings				
Vehicles				
Plant and equipment				
Office furniture and equipment				
(1)				
CURRENT ASSETS:				
Trade debtors				
Stocks				
Cash				
Prepayments				
(2)				
CURRENT LIABILITIES:				
Trade creditors				
Hire purchase creditors				
Dividends				
Taxation				
Other				
(3)				
NET ASSETS (1) + (2) − (3)				
FINANCED BY:				
Share capital				
Capital reserves				
Revenue reserves				
Loans				
Return on capital employed	%	%	%	%
Liquidity ratio				
Sales/capital ratio				

FIGURE 29. Budgeted balance sheet.

Budgeted Balance Sheet for the Year Ending 31 December 1976

	£	£
Fixed assets		
Vehicles at cost	35,000	
less Depreciation	(18,000)	17,000
Other assets at cost	6,500	
less Depreciation	(3,000)	3,500
		20,500
Current assets		
Stock	3,000	
Debtors	7,000	
Bank	5,500	15,500
		36,000
Share capital		20,000
Profit-and-loss-account		3,000
Loan		5,000
Current liabilities		8,000
		36,000

11.4 SUMMARY

1 The success of any business begins at the planning stage. In simple terms, planning is deciding where the company should be in three to five years or more and the strategy required to get it there. The first year of a business plan is expressed in a series of budgets.

2 There are three kinds of budget which are common to most businesses:
  (*a*) The operating budget which is expressed in sales, costs, and profit.
  (*b*) The capital expenditure budget which defines the capital expenditure requirements for the period (or periods).
  (*c*) The cash budget which is principally concerned with the flow of cash in and out of the business.

3 The sales budget, fleet operating budget, workshop budget, and administration budget make up the operating budget, whilst the administration budget is subdivided into departmental (or sectional) budgets (traffic office, accounts office, etc.).

4 The master budget is comprised of all the budgets and is expressed in the form of a profit-and-loss statement and a balance sheet.

5 Actual performance is measured against planned performance via the budgets and management action is taken when deviations emerge. Unless there is such action there is very little point in using budgets.

6 Variations between budgeted and actual performance figures are called *variances*, which are dealt with in Chapter 12.

12 Standard Costing

12.1 THE MEANING OF STANDARD COSTING

We saw in Part Two how costs are obtained and recorded, i.e. the actual costs incurred. While it is of utmost importance for managers to know what it is costing them to run a fleet of vehicles, recorded costs offer no guide as to what the costs *should* have been. Moreover, the only means of cost comparison they offer is that of current costs against previous costs which by itself is pointless, especially if costs were abnormally high or exceptionally low. A way of overcoming this predicament, and of making more sense of costing, is to employ a system of standard costing.

Standard costing is a system which uses *predetermined* costs to which actual costs are compared. The differences between standard and actual costs are known as variances; these are 'analysed' into reasons or causes so that management can take appropriate action to correct adverse situations, a process known as 'variance analysis'. In outline the costs involved are:

1 The standard cost.
2 The actual cost.
3 The variance.

For those who imagine that standard costing is more complex than historical costing the answer is: once standard costs have been set the whole process of recording costs becomes more meaningful. Standard costing is now widely used in the U.S.A. and United Kingdom, and although of particular benefit to manufacturing industries it can nevertheless be put to good use by fleet operators. Moreover, in view of the simplicity of road transport operations – the carrying of goods – standard costing is in this case a fairly straightforward chore.

12.2 VEHICLE STANDARD COSTS

Predetermined – or standard – costs should be set for each class of vehicle having regard to normal or expected operating conditions. When it comes to repair costs it can be argued that they are indeterminable. On the other hand a mature manager should not let that kind of argument prevent him from pursuing his task. If, for example, a particular type of vehicle has been used over a period of time the historical cost records would show the repair costs to date, from which average annual costs could be obtained. The workshop foreman, if he is worth his salt, should know within reason the things that are likely to go wrong with a particular class of vehicle. True he will not know *when*, but here again his assumptions can be evaluated and average annual costs obtained.

The next feature to bear in mind is which costs are *controllable* and which are *uncontrollable*, i.e. where action can and can't be taken when things go wrong, because that is what standard costing is all about. Whether repair costs are controllable is a matter of opinion; in some cases they are (e.g. bad driver and/or maintenance policy, an inefficient workshop), but in other cases they are not (e.g. manufacturing faults).

Standard costs should therefore be set for each class of vehicle having regard to *normal* or expected operating conditions. What is normal for one operator need not be normal for other operators even though the vehicle may be of the same type and class. Type of work, load, terrain, etc., each has an influence on operating costs. An operator should therefore set his own standard costs (as he should fix his own rates) and not confuse the issue by using the costs of other operators, who perhaps are less efficient than himself.

Standard costs should be divided into *fixed* and *variable* costs (and sometimes semi-fixed) following normal costing practice. This division will necessitate setting standard overhead costs for inclusion in vehicle fixed costs (although the treatment should be no different from that described in Chapter 7); this will involve some form of budgeting.

12.2.1 SETTING VEHICLE STANDARD COSTS – VARIABLE

Setting standard costs for individual vehicles is a fairly straightforward task, as outlined below for vehicle ABC123:

(a) Fuel

Factors involved are price of fuel and average kilometres per litre after allowing for contingency factors (work, load, terrain, average speeds, etc.).

Example:

Price of fuel per litre: xp
Average k.p.l.: y
Standard cost per kilometre: zp $(x \div y)$

E

(b) Oil

Factors involved are price of oil and average kilometres per litre.

Example:

Price of oil per litre: xp
Average k.p.l.: y
Standard cost per kilometre: zp $(x \div y)$

(c) Tyres

Factors involved are those already discussed in Part Two, i.e. the price of tyres and average tyre life.

Example:

Price of tyres: £x
Average tyre life: y km
Standard cost per kilometre: zp (£$x \div y$)

(d) Repairs and Maintenance.

Factors involved are service or maintenance costs and estimated repair costs as discussed in section 12.2, derived from workshop rates and outside charges.

Example:

Budgeted annual cost of services and repairs: £x
Budgeted annual kilometres: y km
Standard cost per kilometre: zp (£$x \div y$)

12.2.2 SETTING VEHICLE STANDARD COSTS – FIXED

Fixed costs are compiled in the same way as that described in Part Two. These are:

1 Licences.
2 Insurance.
3 Depreciation.
4 Rent and rates (if applicable).

To complete these time costs, fleet indirect expenses and business overhead apportionments must be added, based on the operating budget described in Chapter 11:

5 Indirect costs.
6 Overhead apportionment.

The total budgeted fixed costs are divided by the budgeted annual vehicle operating hours to arrive at a standard fixed cost per hour.

12.3 STANDARD DRIVER'S WAGES AND EXPENSES

Driver wages costs are based on the basic rate per hour for each grade of driver, the hours employed at basic rate, and the overtime hours at overtime rate.

Example:

Basic hourly rate: xp
Overtime rates:
   (a) Weekdays/Saturdays: yp
   (b) Sundays: zp

The total annual wages cost per vehicle is divided by the vehicle annual *operating* hours to arrive at the standard wages cost per hour:

$$\frac{\text{Annual wages cost per vehicle}}{\text{Vehicle operating hours per annum}} = \frac{\text{Standard wages cost}}{\text{per operating hour}}$$

When driver expenses are known or can be calculated – e.g. tolls, living-out allowance, parking – they should be listed to arrive at an average cost per kilometre or per working day.

12.4 WORKSHOP STANDARD COST RATE

Workshop labour costs are based on basic rates for each grade of employee plus a standard overhead rate covering all workshop expenses as described in Chapter 8. To obtain a standard cost rate the total workshop expense is divided by the net hours to be utilized.

Example:

Total budgeted expense: £x
Activity at n%: y hours
Standard cost rate: £z (£x ÷ y)

The rate should reflect itself in vehicle repair and maintenance costs, but each expense should be controlled by means of the workshop operating statement.

12.5 STANDARD COST SUMMARY

Standard costs should be summarized for each vehicle on a standard cost summary, schedule, or card (*see* Figure 30). The vehicle cost sheet in

STANDARD COST CARD

VEHICLE_____   FLEET No._____

STANDARD ACTIVITY_____ DAYS_____ km per day____ (ANNUAL_____)

	Annual £	Operating day £	Operating hour £	km p
FIXED:				
Licence				
Operating licence				
Insurance				
Depreciation				
Garage*				
Fleet indirect				
Overhead				
VARIABLE:				
Fuel				
Oil				
Tyres				
REPAIRS AND MAINTENANCE:				
Internal				
External				
DRIVER RATES				
Basic				
,, x $1\frac{1}{2}$				
,, x 2				
Expenses				

(* Delete if included with Fleet indirect or Overhead)

FIGURE 30. Standard cost card.

		CURRENT MONTH			YEAR TO DATE		
VEHICLE STANDARD COST SHEET							
REG. No. --------------			MONTH-----------				
FLEET No. --------------							
LOCATION -------------							
	Std. unit cost £	Standard cost £	Actual cost £	Variance £	Standard cost £	Actual cost £	Variance £
FIXED COSTS:							
Road fund licence							
Operating licence							
Insurance							
Depreciation							
Garage							
Fleet indirect							
VARIABLE COSTS:							
Fuel							
Oil							
Tyres							
REP. and .MAINT.:							
Internal							
External							
DRIVER COSTS:							
Wages							
Expenses							
TOTAL COST							
REVENUE							
GROSS PROFIT							
OVERHEADS							
PROFIT/LOSS							
KILOMETRES							
DAYS							
TONNES							

FIGURE 31. Vehicle standard cost sheet.

Figure 31 incorporates standard costs which would emanate from the standard cost summary, schedule, or card.

12.6 STANDARD RATES

Standard rates are normally based on total costs plus the desired profit, having regard to the capital invested, risk factors (as described in Chapter 11), and sales volumes as laid down in the sales budget. Standard rates can be expressed in any form – per tonne, pack, litre, etc. – depending on the type of traffic carried.

Example:

Vehicle: ABC123
Standard cost per unit: £x
Budgeted sales per annum (units × rate): y × £x

Note: Where it is known that a vehicle's standard rate will vary according to the type of traffic carried during the year, the budgeted traffic and sales for each type of vehicle should be separately stated if sense is to be made of standard costing and variance analysis.

12.7 VARIANCES

12.7.1 REASONS FOR VARIABLE VARIANCES

The most common reasons for variable variances are price and usage. Because fuel, oil, tyres, and maintenance costs are based on known or anticipated prices, consumption, and time factors, variances are bound to occur where either price or usage varies from that laid down as standard. Examples are given below. The standard costs shown are, of course, imaginary.

(a) Fuel

Example:

Distance covered: 650 km
Standard price of fuel: 4·0p per km
Actual price of fuel: 4·2p per km
Actual fuel consumed: £28·80
Standard consumption:

Actual kilometres (650) at *standard* cost (4·0p)	£26·00
less Actual consumption at *actual* cost	£28·80
Total variance – *unfavourable*	(£2·80)

The total variance is therefore £2.80, made up as follows:

Price variance: 650 km at 4·2p *less* 4·0p	£1·30
Usage variance: difference between total and price variances	£1·50
	£2·80

Note carefully that standard and actual costs are based on the *actual* kilometres covered.

Price changes are normally reflected in revised standard costs, but if fuel is bought on the road price variations are bound to occur. The usage variance could be due to a variety of reasons (a heavy foot, poor maintenance, etc.) which would call for investigation.

(b) Oil

Price and usage variances are calculated in the same way as for fuel.

(c) Tyres

Price variances will occur when, for example, it becomes necessary to replace a tyre from sources other than a company's central buying service, or when price increases are not reflected in revised standard costs. A usage variance will arise where a tyre does not last or exceeds its standard life.

(d) Repairs and Maintenance

The difference between the standard repair and maintenance cost per kilometre and the actual cost will be the result of the incidence of repair and maintenance work and the costs involved. The difference will therefore be an *expenditure* variance. As already stated, workshop costs can be controlled internally whereas external work cannot be so controlled; for that reason it is best to separate internal from external costs.

12.7.2 REASONS FOR FIXED VARIANCES

Vehicle fixed costs such as licences, insurance, and depreciation seldom change during the year, and when they do the obvious step is to revise the standard costs – which after all is correct seeing that standard costs are concerned with what costs *should be*. Where costs are not revised the differences will be an expenditure variance.

When it comes to fleet indirect costs and business overheads the position is slightly more complex because absorption depends on two factors: charges to customers and the level of expenses incurred. The difference between standard and actual costs in this case can therefore be due to an expenditure variance (expenses being more or less than standard) or to a volume variance (the actual number of operating or absorption hours being more or less than standard). This is illustrated below for vehicle ABC 123.

Example:

Budgeted fixed overhead for month (including licences, insurance, etc.): £400
Budgeted operating hours for month: 200
Standard cost per hour: £2
Actual fixed overhead for month: £430
Actual operating hours for month: 190

Overhead total variance

Actual cost incurred		£430
less Standard cost incurred (190 × £2)		(£380)
Total overhead variance – unfavourable		£50

Total overhead variance

1 *Expenditure variance*

Actual cost incurred	£430
less Standard cost as per budget	(£400)
Unfavourable variance	£30

2 *Volume variance:*

Budgeted hours at standard (200 × £2)	£400
less Actual hours at standard (190 × £2)	(£380)
Unfavourable variance	£20

The company in question has therefore lost out on two counts:

1 It has spent more than it should have done – £30 more.
2 It has under-absorbed ten hours of overheads from vehicle operations.

The fixed-overhead variance analysis is therefore:

Expenditure variance	£30
Volume variance	£20
Total variance	£50

The reasons for the expenditure variance would be obtained from the operating statements which set out budgeted and actual expenditure by type of expense.

12.7.3 REASONS FOR SALES VARIANCES

When the rates charged differ from those laid down as standard the difference is a sales price (or rates) variance. Similarly, when the actual volume of traffic differs from that laid down in the sales budget the difference is a sales volume (or quantity) variance. This is illustrated below for vehicle ABC123.

Example:

Total sales variance

		£
Budgeted sales for month:		
500 units at £2·00 per unit		1,000
less Actual sales for month:		
250 units at £2·00 per unit	£500	
200 units at £1·80 per unit	£360	
	£860	(860)
Total sales variance – unfavourable		140

Sales price variance

	£
Standard sale (450 units* at £2·00)	900
less Actual sales	(860)
Sales price variance (200 × £0·20)	40

(**actual* quantities sold at standard rate)

Sales quantity variance

	£
Quantity variance:	
500 − 450 = 50*	
Sales quantity variance:	
50 units at £2·00 per unit	100

*budgeted quantity less actual quantity)

	£
Sales analysis of variances	
Price variance	40
Quantity variance	100
Total variance	140

Revenue and profit have therefore been reduced on two counts: less units were carried than planned; and of the units carried there was a reduction in the traffic rate, resulting in a reduction in profit.

12.8 VARIANCE ANALYSIS

The simple cost sheet in Figure 31 shows both current and cumulative cost variances. It does not, however, show the reasons for the variances nor whether they are controllable or uncontrollable. It is therefore necessary to analyse the variances in more detail, either on a separate variance analysis summary or perhaps on an integrated vehicle cost statement, under such headings as price, usage, expenditure, quantity, and volume variances, as described.

12.9 SUMMARY

1 Standard costing is a system which uses predetermined costs and prices to which actual costs and prices are compared. Standard costs are what costs ought to be under normal operating conditions having regard to planned activity, time, and usage; actual costs are the actual costs incurred; the differences between the two are called variances.

2 Variances can be either favourable or unfavourable; the type of variance is apparent (e.g. price, usage, expenditure, quantity) but not the reason for its existence. The latter calls for investigation.

3 Standard costs are set for vehicle variable and fixed costs, drivers' wages, workship fixed and variable costs, and fleet and business overheads, while standard rates and volumes are set for sales or turnover.

4 In simple terms, standard costing is cost planning and calls for action when significant deviations from the standard occur.

13 Break-even Analysis and Marginal Costing

13.1 BREAK-EVEN ANALYSIS

13.1.1 DEFINITION

Break-even analysis is the process of ascertaining the effect on profit of variations in the volume of activity. Briefly, it relates costs and profits for various activities and demonstrates the point at which an enterprise 'breaks even', there being no profit and no loss.

13.1.2 FIXED AND VARIABLE COSTS

It was shown in Part Two that costs can have different characteristics; some costs depend on *time* (e.g. fixed costs) while others depend on *activity* (e.g. variable costs). At the same time there are costs which are a bit of each; these are called semi-fixed (or semi-variable or mixed) costs. If we look again at vehicle costs we see at once the fixed element, made up of road licences, insurance, etc., and the variable element, made up of fuel, oil, tyres, and maintenance. Together these costs make up the total cost.

Again it should be stressed that no cost is truly fixed in the full meaning of the word. From the costing point of view, however, fixed costs are fixed in the sense that they remain the same irrespective of the level of activity. Regarding vehicle costs, the fixed costs are there whether the vehicle is driven 50,000 km during the year or a mere 500 km. This same principle applies to administration costs, most of which are fixed in the short term.

The importance of distinguishing between fixed and variable costs is fundamental if break-even analysis is to be understood and applied. This can be seen from the following illustration.

Example:

An additional vehicle is purchased by I. Towem Ltd to cover the work arising from a new contract with a self-service grocery chain. Vehicle fixed costs are £3,000. After the first month's operation the vehicle's cost sheet shows the following:

Revenue	£900
less Costs	(£690)
Profit	£210

Although the transport manager may clap his hands in glee he should quickly realize that the profit of £210 is on paper only, and that until the fixed costs of £3,000 are fully recovered in addition to the variable costs for every kilometre run, the operation cannot possibly show true profit. In short, until the vehicle passes the break-even point (when costs equate with income) no profit will be made. The questions which must then be asked are:

1 When will the vehicle break even?
2 At what *sales* level?
3 At what *activity*?

13.1.3 THE NEEDS FOR ANALYSIS

We need to know the time (fixed) and activity (variable) costs, the various levels of activity, and the sales income arising from them. Activity levels should be expressed in relation to time (i.e. months) thus showing *when* the vehicle would break even.

Example:

The above vehicle's fixed costs are made up of annual costs (£1,200), apportioned overheads (£500), and driver's wages which are treated as fixed (£1,300): a total of £3,000. Variable costs are 7p per km. The total annual activity is expected to be 40,000 km, and the annual revenue £7,000. *Note:* the vehicle will cover a fairly regular route and the schedule will show the number of kilometres the vehicle is expected to cover in every operating week; the 40,000 km is the sum total of these kilometres.

The transport manager is required to calculate the vehicle's break-even point in terms of revenue, activity, and time. While the problem can be solved mathematically the easiest way to tackle it is by means of a graph.

13.1.4 THE BREAK-EVEN CHART

(*a*) *Description*

The break-even chart is a very useful device for showing the relationship between costs and profit. It is nothing more that three lines (or curves) on a sheet of paper representing fixed and variable costs and revenue. The horizontal axis is expressed in units (e.g. kilometres, tonnes, litres, packs) and the vertical axis in money. The traditional break-even chart shows the fixed-cost curve as a straight line (sometimes with steps when fixed costs

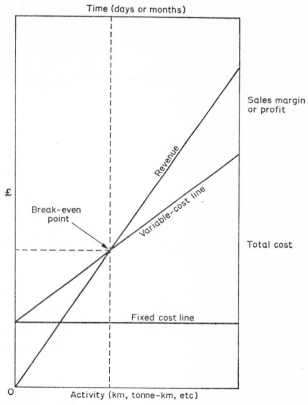

FIGURE 32. Break-even chart (1).

change – *see* section 13.17) on the horizontal axis in line with the cost level shown on the verticle axis, and the variable-cost curve as a diagonal line sloping away from the fixed-cost curve at nil activity (*see* Figure 32). The variable-cost curve is, in fact, the total-cost curve as it is placed upon the fixed-cost curve (fixed cost plus variable cost = total cost). The revenue curve is a diagonal line from the point of origin (where the vertical and horizontal axes meet) through the total-cost curve to the right-hand vertical. The point where the revenue curve crosses the total-cost curve is the break-even point.

(b) *Compiling a break-even chart*

Using the figures in section 13.1.3 the break-even chart can be compiled as follows:

1 Analyse all costs under fixed and variable, and determine the units and revenue relating to them.
2 Obtain a sheet of graph paper, select a suitable scale, and mark off the vertical axis in pounds and the horizontal axis in units (kilometres, tonnes, etc.).
3 Using the vertical scale, mark off the fixed-cost level (£3,000) and draw a horizontal line.

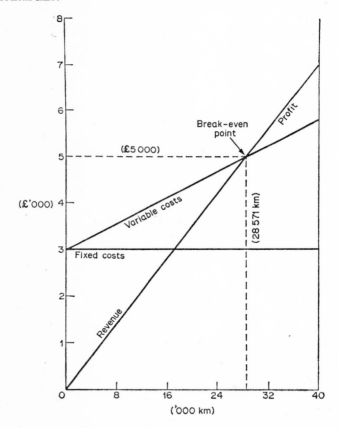

Notes:
1 Fixed costs, £3,000; variable costs, £2,800 (40,000 km at 7p per km); revenue, £7,000.
2 As the volume of fixed costs is high the vehicle will not break even until it has covered 28,571 km, break-even revenue being £5,000 (*see* section 13.1.5).

FIGURE 33. Break-even chart (2).

4 Using the vertical scale again, determine the total-cost level by adding the variable costs (40,000 × 7p = £2,800) to the fixed costs (£3,000) – making a total of £5,800. Draw a diagonal line from the fixed-cost curve at nil activity.
5 Obtain the sales figure, mark off the sales level on the vertical scale, and draw a diagonal to it from the point of origin.

The finished product can be seen in Figure 33. It shows the vehicle break-even point at £5,000 sales and 28,571 km. The transport manager can now look up the vehicle's schedule to ascertain the approximate break-even date.

(c) *Alternative break-even chart*

An alternative form of chart is shown in Figure 34, it uses the variable-

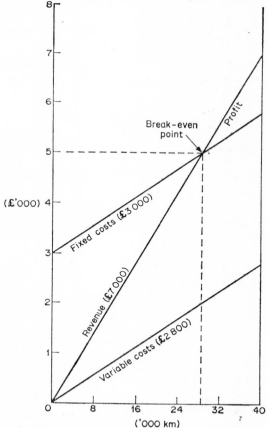

FIGURE 34. Break-even chart (3).

cost curve as a base. This presentation has the advantage of showing that below the break-even point it is the fixed costs that are not being recovered.

13.1.5 BREAK-EVEN MATHEMATICS

Besides the graphical method of computing the break-even point it can also be computed by means of the formulae described below. The first formula gives the break-even sales from which the break-even units can be calculated; the second formula gives the break-even units (or activity).

$$\frac{\text{Sales} \times \text{Fixed costs}}{\text{Sales} - \text{Variable costs}} = \text{Break-even point} \qquad (1)$$

Using the figures in section 13.1.3 we get:

$$\frac{7,000 \times 3,000}{7,000 - 2,800} = \frac{21,000,000}{4,200} = £5,000 \text{ break-even sales}$$

We can calculate the break-even kilometres by taking the break-even sales of £5,000, deducting the fixed costs, and dividing the resultant by the variable costs per kilometre (7p):

Break-even sales	£5,000	
less Fixed costs	(£3,000)	
Variable costs	£2,000	(or 200,000p)

$$\text{Break-even kilometres} = \frac{200,000}{7} = 28,571 \text{ km (nearest)}$$

The calculation is rather long-winded, however, which brings us to the second formula:

$$\frac{\text{Fixed costs}}{\text{Selling value} - \text{Unit variable cost}} = \text{Break-even point} \qquad (2)$$

If the selling price (or rate) per kilometre was 17·5p the calculation would be:

$$\frac{300,000}{17\cdot5 - 7\cdot0} = \frac{300,000}{10\cdot5} = 28,571 \text{ km}$$

The proof of this calculation is:

Sales (28,571 × 17·5p)	£5,000
less Variable costs (28,571 × 7.0p)	(£2,000)
Fixed costs	£3,000

13.1.6 THE POINT OF BREAKING EVEN

The vehicle that does not break even over its trading year is something of a threat to a business, particularly if the fleet is small. The same applies to groups of vehicles within a large fleet. The business that barely breaks even or makes only a moderate surplus is doomed to failure sooner or later.

Although we have related the break-even chart to a vehicle it can and should be applied to all facets of a business: to groups of vehicles, departments, depots, branches, and entire company operations. Break-even charts are therefore of invaluable assistance in profit planning – in determining the prices or rates to be charged and the level of activity needed to achieve the desired profit. Moreover, where expansion or an increase in fixed costs is envisaged it is important for management to know what effect the change will have on the break-even point and profits.

13.1.7 GUIDE IN DECISION MAKING

Management should always be aware of the break-even point in any situation involving costs and profits, as break-even analysis provides an excellent guide in decision making. In fairness it must be pointed out that not all situations are so simple as the vehicle illustration described above. Some difficulties are:

1 The separation of semi-fixed (or semi-variable or mixed) costs into fixed and variable can be a difficult process involving statistical analysis (e.g. scattergraphs and least squares).
2 Fixed costs may not stay fixed, e.g. where activity is increased by shift working involving the employment of an extra driver as well as additional administrative overheads to cater for the increased turnover. In this case the increases should be brought in as steps on the fixed-cost curve at the appropriate activity.
3 Activity may vary for reasons outside the control of management (e.g. strikes, breakdown, market changes).
4 Sales may vary as the result of differential rates, fall-off in volume, etc.

Nevertheless, break-even charts provide an excellent short-term guide – and a guide only – in profit planning and decision making.

13.2 MARGINAL COSTING

Marginal costing is an extension of break-even analysis but has the emphasis on the variable or *marginal* costs.

13.2.1 DEFINITION AND THEORY

The marginal cost is the additional cost of running an extra kilometre, i.e. the variable cost. As already stated, fixed costs are fixed (in the short term) whether a vehicle runs 50,000 km or 500 km per annum. The additional costs involved are therefore the variable costs. The theory is that the difference between the selling price (or traffic rate) per unit (kilometre, tonne, etc.) and the variable or *marginal* cost per unit contributes to company fixed overheads and profit, in that order. The transport manager is, however, more concerned with total marginal costs rather than with unit costs, and with total revenue from a job or contract. Fixed costs are therefore disregarded because it is the marginal costs that really matter.

Example:

A manager has the choice of undertaking one of two contracts – he cannot do both. The vehicle fixed costs are the same for each case. The revenue and marginal costs involved are:

	Contract A £	Contract B £
Revenue	8,000	7,000
less Variable (marginal) costs:		
Fuel and oil ⎫		
Tyres ⎬	(4,300)	(2,900)
Maintenance ⎪		
Variable overheads ⎭		
Contribution	3,700	4,100

Although Contract B has the smallest revenue it is nevertheless the most profitable, because it generates the biggest contribution towards the company's fixed overheads and profit.

13.2.2 TERMINOLOGY

There are two basic terms:

1 *Marginal cost* comprises all direct costs (fuel and oil, tyres, and repairs and maintenance) and variable overhead. Variable overhead comprises those overheads that are strictly variable, i.e. incurred as a result of a job or activity.
2 *Contribution* is, the difference between the selling price (or rate) and the marginal cost. It is made up of fixed cost and profit, i.e. fixed cost before the break-even point and profit after the break-even point. *Note*: contribution is sometimes referred to as 'marginal profit' which is not a strictly correct definition.

13.2.3 CONTRIBUTION

(a) The concept of contribution

Exponents of marginal costing argue that to apportion business overheads over products, services, and operations is a completely misleading exercise, no matter how scientific the apportionments may be. It is known as the traditional or total-cost approach. Consider the following:

Vehicle	Turnover	Total cost	Net profit
	£	£	£
1	13,000	14,000	(1,000)
2	27,000	29,000	(2,000)
3	18,000	13,000	5,000
4	12,000	8,000	4,000
5	16,000	16,000	—
6	14,000	10,000	4,000
	100,000	90,000	10,000

The impression given by the net profit statement is that vehicles 1, 2, and 5 are completely unprofitable, and that vehicles 3, 4, and 6 are carrying the most profitable traffic. This is because the total cost includes fixed expenses which have been apportioned on some basis favoured by the company's management. If we now eliminate *all* fixed expenses from the total cost and show marginal costs only, we see quite a different state of affairs:

Vehicle	Turnover	Marginal cost	Contribution
	£	£	£
1	13,000	7,000	6,000
2	27,000	14,000	13,000
3	18,000	9,500	8,500
4	12,000	5,500	6,500
5	16,000	8,750	7,250
6	14,000	6,250	7,750
	100,000	51,000	49,000
		less Fixed costs	(39,000)
		Net profit	10,000

Now it can be seen that vehicles 1, 2, and 5 make a total contribution of £26,250 towards the company's fixed costs and profit. If these three vehicles were eliminated and only vehicles 3, 4, and 6 were employed, the position would result in a loss, as shown overleaf.

Contribution may therefore be expressed as follows: Sales — Marginal costs = Contribution = Fixed cost + Profit.

What has been said so far is really an extension of the need for costing discussed in Chapter 4.

Vehicle	Turnover £	Marginal cost £	Contribution £
1	—	—	—
2	—	—	—
3	18,000	9,500	8,500
4	12,000	5,500	6,500
5	—	—	—
6	14,000	6,250	7,750
	44,000	21,250	22,750

	less Fixed costs	(32,000)*
	Net loss	(9,250)

(* Fixed costs have been reduced by £7,000, which represents those vehicle fixed costs which have been eliminated with vehicles 1, 2, and 5 plus a proportion of administrative expenses.)

(b) 'Net' Contribution.

There is no reason why the marginal-cost statement should not be modified by introducing *vehicle* fixed costs on the statement, i.e. by adjusting the contribution by each vehicle's fixed costs (which include *direct* fixed costs such as licenses, insurance, etc., but not apportioned costs). These are, after all, direct costs and their deduction is right and proper. The marginal-cost statement then becomes:

Vehicle	Turnover £	Marginal cost £	Contribution £	Direct fixed costs £	Net Contribution £
1	13,000	7,000	6,000	2,000	4,000
2	27,000	14,000	13,000	3,000	10,000
3	18,000	9,500	8,500	2,000	6,500
4	12,000	5,500	6,500	1,500	5,000
5	16,000	8,750	7,250	2,000	5,250
6	14,000	6,250	7,750	1,250	6,500
	100,000	51,000	49,000	11,750	37,250

	less Fixed costs	(27,250)
	Net profit	10,000

The 'net contribution' presentation is therefore a truer reflection of the facts – which is the sole purpose of management accounts – and should be used in transport operations.

13.2.4 DECISION MAKING AND PROFIT PLANNING

Marginal costing is a valuable tool for decision making and profit planning. Besides determining which traffic and vehicle operations provide the highest contribution and should therefore be continued, it also highlights the effect on profit of such factors as the taking on of new contracts, the employment of extra vehicles and drivers, decisions on buy and lease, the reduction or increase of prices, and so on, while assisting managers with their day-to-day operations.

Example:

A farmer wishes to move some cattle to another farm and approaches a haulier who quotes a price of £20. The farmer complains that he is prepared to pay £10 but beyond that would rather walk his cattle than pay the full price. As both vehicle and driver are *idle* the haulier has already quoted a price with a small profit. His price is made up of £6 variable costs, £2 profit, and £12 fixed costs. The farmer's offer of £10 is therefore below total cost, and rather than lose £8 the haulier turns down the job. Is he right?

The point here is that both vehicle and driver are idle. The fixed cost of £12 is incurred whether the vehicle runs or not. The variable cost of moving the cattle is £6, therefore any income received in *excess* of this figure would contribute to the fixed expenses, in this case £4.

Sales	—	Marginal cost	=	Contribution	—	Fixed cost	=	Reduced fixed cost
£10		£6		£4		£12		£8

The haulier has therefore made a wrong decision. Had he understood the meaning of contribution the error would not have been made.

13.2.5 *Profit/volume ratio*

From the formulae in section 13.1.5 an important ratio arises. If we express selling price as a ratio of the contribution the resultant figure is called the profit/volume ratio. Expressed as a formula it is:

$$\text{Profit/volume ratio} = \frac{\text{Contribution}}{\text{Selling price}}$$

Using the same figures we get:

$$\text{P/V ratio} = \frac{10 \cdot 50}{17 \cdot 50} = \text{£}0 \cdot 60 \text{ per unit}$$

Using the profit/volume ratio we can quickly calculate the contribution for any given sales level. For example:

£7,000 sales × £0·60 per unit = £4,200 contribution

(Proof: £7,000 sales less £2,800 variable costs.)

13.3 SUMMARY

1 Break-even analysis is the process of ascertaining the effect on profit of variations in the volume of activity. It takes cognizance of the fact that costs have different characteristics. Some costs are affected by *time* (i.e. fixed costs) while others are affected by activity (i.e. variable costs). The importance of distinguishing between fixed and variable costs is fundamental if break-even analysis is to be understood.

2 The break-even point (of a company, department, cost-centre, etc.) is the point where income equates with expenditure, there being no profit and no loss. One method of computing the break-even point is by means of a break-even chart (*see* Figure 32), or it can be calculated. Break-even analysis is essential for decision-making purposes, e.g. in price fixing.

3 Marginal costing is an extension of break-even analysis but places the emphasis on the variable or *marginal* costs. The theory is that the difference between the selling price (or traffic rate) and the variable costs *contributes* to company fixed costs and profit, in that order. Expressed as a formula it is:

Sales — Variable (marginal) costs = Fixed costs + Profit

In practice there is no profit until all fixed costs have been recovered from sales income.

4 The profit/volume ratio is important for pricing and profit purposes. It is obtained by dividing the contribution by the selling price (or traffic rate). When multiplied by the sales volume it gives the contribution for any sales level, thus assisting in price and profit planning.

14 Vehicle Replacement and Comparative Costs

Before a vehicle is replaced or a fleet of vehicles is extended, an analysis should be made to ensure that the replacement/acquisition is really necessary. It could be that as the result of re-routeing, etc., a company could manage without replacing a vehicle or acquiring an extra one. On the other hand, where such action is necessary an analysis should be made of the various types of vehicles available to ensure that the right type of vehicle is obtained. To blindly replace a vehicle with one of the same type, without giving thought to alternatives, could be foolhardy. Factors which should be taken into account are capital outlay and running costs, payload, vehicle life including depreciation and maintenance, and timing (i.e. when to buy). This chapter, however, is mainly concerned with the costing aspect of replacement alternatives, and we therefore assume that a vehicle replacement policy has already been established.

14.1 METHODS OF VEHICLE REPLACEMENT

These are: purchase for cash, buy on hire purchase, leasing, and contract hire. It is often said that the first method – purchase for cash – is the best and cheapest in the long run. In fact the statement is true only where a company has adequate funds available. Hire purchase is an obvious alternative where funds are tight. Leasing and contract hire are complete alternatives; they are similar in so far as the vehicle leased or hired does not become the property of the lessee/hirer, but they differ in both principle and cost.

14.1.1 PURCHASE FOR CASH

This is the simplest method and requires little explanation. If a replacement takes place a sum of money, equal to the delivered price of the new vehicle less an allowance for the old vehicle, is handed over and the buyer assumes full responsibility for the new vehicle. Although the new owner has to meet all operating costs, including maintenance, he enjoys the benefits of ownership (he can sell the vehicle if he so wishes), of the manufacturer's warranty for twelve months, and of certain tax allowances (*see* section 14.2 which are synonymous with ownership.

14.1.2 BUY ON HIRE PURCHASE

This method has the advantage that large sums of money are retained within the business, thus enhancing the working-capital position. A number of companies have found themselves in financial difficulty by not adopting this method of acquisition, when all that was needed was a little fore-thought and planning. The disadvantages are the cost of borrowing and the fact that ownership is not immediate. The same tax advantages accrue, however, as when the vehicle is bought outright.

14.1.3 LEASING

Under a leasing contract the lessee agrees to pay to the leasing company at regular intervals (usually monthly) a sum of money which is geared to the cash price of the vehicle. Although leasing contracts vary the contract is usually fixed for a number of years, known as the 'primary period', after which time the lessee may purchase the vehicle for a nominal sum.

Example:

Vehicle life: 5 years
Cash price of vehicle: £2,500 (including tyres)
Term of lease: 5 years
Monthly rental at (say) £24 per £1,000: £60
Total rental over 5 years: 60 × £60 = £3,600

Besides an annual rental the lessee is responsible for all operating costs, including repairs and maintenance. Depreciation does not, of course, enter into it because the lessee does not own the vehicle. All operating costs, including the rental, are allowable for tax purposes, while the writing-down (or annual) allowance on the capital expenditure of the vehicle is said to be passed on to the lessee by way of reduced rental.

14.1.4 CONTRACT HIRE

Here again contract hire terms vary considerably. Generally speaking the contract hire charge usually covers vehicle rental based on capital cost and profit, annual vehicle fixed expenses, and a kilometre charge based on a minimum annual kilometres, sometimes excluding fuel and oil. In the case of breakdown the hire company undertakes the repair of the vehicle and supplies a replacement vehicle. In short, the contract hire company supplies the vehicle taxed and insured, undertakes all repair and maintenance and supplies a replacement vehicle as required. The advantage to fleet operators is that costs are known in advance. The disadvantage is cost, often high.

Lease or contract hire?

Contract hire is usually more expensive than leasing in view of the service given. A small operator with little capital and no workshop facilities or administrative staff may favour contract hire, although consideration should be given to the location of the hire company's service centre, the type of vehicle supplied, the cash flow situation, and so on. The best plan would be to draw up a comparative-cost table for both methods, consider the factors given above, and decide accordingly.

14.2 TAX CONSIDERATIONS

In considering alternatives, whether to buy, lease, or hire, the effect of taxation should be taken into account. Besides vehicle operating expenses which are allowable for tax purposes there are certain capital allowances which go hand in glove with ownership. These are the first-year allowance of 80 per cent (on expenditure incurred between 20 July 1971 and 31 July 1973 inclusive, which is subject to legislation)* and the annual writing-down allowance of 25 per cent which is calculated on each year's reducing balance. Corporation tax at the time of writing is 40 per cent. The effect of taxation on a vehicle can be seen from the following example:

Example:

Suppose a vehicle costs £2,500 (including tyres) and has a life of five years. With allowances at the percentages given above, the tax allowances and savings are:

	£	Allowance £	Corporation tax at 40% £	Tax saving £
Purchase price	2,500		1,000	
less First-year allowance	(2,000)	2,000		
Written-down value Year 1	500		200	800
less Writing-down allowance	(125)	125		
Written-down value Year 2	375		150	50
less Writing-down allowance	(94)	94		
Written-down value Year 3	281		113	37
less Writing-down allowance	(70)	70		
Written-down value Year 4	211		85	28
less Writing-down allowance	(53)	53		
Written-down value Year 5	158		64	21
		2,342		936

* Now agreed at 80 per cent 20 July 1971–21 March 1972; 100 per cent on or after 22 March 1972. Either rate may be claimed after 22.3.72 but no writing-down allowance is available in the latter case, i.e. 100 per cent.

Over the commercial life of the vehicle the sum of £2,342 would be set against profits by way of capital allowances. If the vehicle was sold at the end of Year 5 for, say, £400 there would be a balancing *charge* of £97 (242 × 40 per cent), which would reduce the tax saving to £839. But if the vehicle was sold for £100 there would be a balancing *allowance* of £23 (£58 × 40 per cent), which would increase the overall allowance to £959.

The matter does not end there because vehicle operating expenditure is also allowable against profits – i.e. fixed and variable costs including drivers' wages and expenses and business overheads. The table in section 14.3 shows total comparative costs over a vehicle's life with the capital and operating allowances given at the bottom.

14.3 COST COMPARISON TABLE

The figures in the example below are for illustrative purposes only and do not reflect current leasing and contract hire charges. As already stated, leasing and contract hire terms vary considerably; it therefore pays to shop around to find the most favourable terms.

Example:

Vehicle: XYZ
Purchase price: £2,500 (including tyres, £240)
Estimated life: 5 years
Annual kilometres: 40,000 km
Tyre life: 24,000 km
Fuel and oil: under contract hire, 6p per km; otherwise 2·5p per km
Repairs and maintenance: £600 per annum
Residual value: £200
Leasing charges: £720 per annum, the lessee bearing all fixed and variable costs (except depreciation)
Contract hire charges: £1,300 per annum plus 6p per km
Other fixed vehicle costs: as shown below

	Purchase £	Hire purchase £	Lease £	Contract hire £
Fixed costs				
Licences	140	140	140	—
Insurance	190	190	190	—
Depreciation	412	412	—	—
Overheads	700	700	700	700
Hire purchase interest	—	120	—	—
Leasing charge	—	—	720	—
Contract hire	—	—	—	1,300
	1,442	1,562	1,750	2,000

		Purchase £	Hire purchase £	Lease £	Contact hire £
Variable costs					
Fuel and oil	2·5p				
Tyres	1·0p				
Repairs and maintenance	1·5p				
40,000 km @	5·0p	2,000	2,000	2,000	—
Contract hire 6p per km		—	—	—	2,400
		3,442	3,562	3,750	4,400
Driver costs					
Wages and expenses		1,400	1,400	1,400	1,400
Total annual costs		4,842	4,962	5,150	5,800
5-year costs		24,210	24,810	25,750	29,000
less Residual value		(200)	(200)	—	—
		24,010	24,610	25,750	29,000
Less Tax allowances:					
Capital allowances ⎱ Allowable expenses ⎰		(9,780)	(10,200)	(10,300)	(11,600)
Comparative net costs		14,230	14,410	15,450	17,400

Notes:

1 Hire purchase interest and leasing and contract hire charges are imaginary.
2 Overheads must be recovered from vehicle operations whether vehicles belong to a company or not.
3 In computing tax allowances, depreciation shown by a company must be written back because only the official Inland Revenue allowances will apply. The computations are as below:

			£	£	£	£
Capital allowances (*see* section 14.2)			2,342	2,342	—	—
less Written-down value	£158		—	—	—	—
Residual value	£200					
	(£42)		(42)	(42)	—	—
		(1)	2,300	2,300	—	—
Allowable expenses			24,210	24,810	25,750	29,000
less Depreciation (5 × £412)			(2,060)	(2,060)	—	—
		(2)	22,150	22,750	25,750	29,000
Total (1) + (2)			24,450	25,050	25,750	29,000
Corporation tax at 40%			9,780	10,200	10,300	11,600

14.4 SUMMARY

1 Vehicles can be acquired by purchase for cash or on hire purchase, leased, or hired.
2 Although outright purchase is the cheapest in the long run the choice very much depends on a company's liquidity position and its vehicle replacement policy.
3 Vehicle ownership attracts certain capital allowances which are not enjoyed if a vehicle is leased or hired. These are at present a first-year allowance of 80 per cent and an annual writing-down allowance of 25 per cent. Vehicle operating expenses, including driver wages, are allowable whether a vehicle is owned or not.
4 Comparative-cost tables show at a glance the financial merits and demerits of buying, leasing, and hiring.
5 The difference between buying for cash and buying on hire purchase is, of course, the interest.
6 In the illustration given leasing charges include *all* variable charges. In practice this would depend on the terms of the contract.

15 Capital Investment Appraisal

Any decision to invest in new projects (e.g. a workshop, a warehouse, extra vehicles, or a completely new depot) calls for careful planning because such a decision will obviously tie up funds for a very long time. It seems to many road transport operators that there is little need to appraise capital investments other than to ensure that each investment contributes to overheads and profit. Such a philosophy can only be true in the short term, whereas it is the long term that really matters. A mature management will therefore want to know the kind of return that can be expected over the life of the project, as part of their profit-planning policy. This chapter sets out to explain in brief terms some of the methods that can be used in investment appraisal.

15.1 METHODS OF APPRAISAL

These are based on:

1 Payback.
2 Average rate of return on investment.
3 Discounted cash flow (the net present value and discounted yield methods).

The first considers the time an investment will take to pay for itself; the second, the average return per annum over the life of the investment; the third, the present value of future net cash flows and yield. The first two methods have been widely used in one form or another in manufacturing industries, but it is only in recent years that the benefits to be derived from the use of discounted cash flow have been realized.

15.2 TERMINOLOGY

Before considering the three methods it is important to understand the meaning of certain basic terms:

1 *Cash flow*: the movement of cash in and out of an enterprise.
2 *Net cash flow*: the difference between cash received and cash paid. When

cash received exceeds cash paid there is a *positive* cash flow; when the reverse, a *negative* cash flow.

3 *Timing:* refers to the timing of net cash flows, i.e. *when* money will be received.

4 *Present value*: the present value of £1 at the commencement of a project

5 *Discounting*: applies to future net cash flows which are discounted to the present value of money.

15.3 PROFIT FORECASTING

The attempt to determine which capital projects are the most profitable must, of course, be preceded by a considerable amount of forecasting. It is necessary to know:

1 Capital cost of each project.
2 Life of each project.
3 Annual operating costs (wages, vehicle expenses, etc.).
4 Annual income.
5 Cost of capital or required rate of return.

Each amount is expressed in cash, and book items such as depreciation and other provisions are ignored as they do not represent cash payments taxation does, however, and is therefore included. The importance of accurate forecasting cannot be overemphasized, because if the forecast were incorrect then the whole exercise would be a complete waste of time For this reason it is often necessary for the accountant and engineer to work jointly on project forecasting.

15.4 PAYBACK METHOD

The objective of the payback method is to ascertain at what period in time a project will have paid for itself, i.e. when net income will equal the initial cash outlay. If, for example, the outlay for a new depot was £100,000 and the cumulative net receipts over the first six years were £102,000, the investment would pay for itself in something less than six years. The formula is

$$\frac{\text{Cash outlay}}{\text{Annual cash returns}} = \text{Payback (years)}$$

Example:

Suppose a manager is confronted with the choice of two alternatives, A and B. The first alternative is a five-year contract with a large retail company which has branches all over the country; the second is also a five-year contract but with a large steel works in South Wales. Both contracts involve the carriage of goods, and they require different types of vehicles. The forecast cash flows drawn up by the accountant in co-operation with the chief engineer are:

	Contract A £	Contract B £
Capital outlay	50,000	50,000
Net cash flow: Year 1	7,000	6,000
Year 2	14,000	20,000
Year 3	21,000	16,000
Year 4	8,000	14,000
Year 5	20,000	8,000
	70,000	64,000
Payback	4 years	3½ years

Contract B would pay for itself in just over 3½ years whereas contract A would take 4 years. Although the difference in this case is marginal, managers who use this method would probably go for contract B.

5.4.1 DISADVANTAGES OF PAYBACK

The payback method has three major weaknesses:

It fails to take account of cash flows *after* the payback period has been reached. In the above example the total net cash flows are £70,000 and £64,000. Contract A is therefore the most profitable but contract B would nevertheless be chosen.

The timing of receipts is ignored. Although contract A is the more profitable of the two, contract B brings in cash receipts of £26,000 over the first two years of the contract compared with contract A's £21,000 for the same period – a difference of £5,000. The importance of liquidity has already been stressed, so contract B should be chosen for this reason alone rather than for payback. Note also that the first two years' forecasts are likely to be more accurate than those of the last three.

It fails to take account of the effect of taxation.

5.5 AVERAGE RATE OF RETURN ON INVESTMENT METHOD

This method determines the average return per annum as a percentage of the initial outlay. The formula is:

$$\frac{\text{Average return per annum}}{\text{Initial outlay}} \times 100 = \text{Average return (\%)}$$

Using the same figures as in section 15.4 we get:

	Contract A	Contract B
Total net cash flow	£70,000	£64,000
Average return per annum ($\div 5$)	£14,000	£12,800
Capital outlay	£50,000	£50,000
Average return per annum	28·0%	25·6%

Reverting to the accounting assessment of profitability and bringing in depreciation over the life of each contract, we get:

	Contract A	Contract B
Average return per annum	£14,000	£12,800
less Straight-line depreciation	(£10,000)	(£10,000)
Average annual profit	£ 4,000	£ 2,800
Average return per annum	8·0%	5·6%

If the returns were based on the *average* capital outlay over the contractual lives (i.e. £50,000 ÷ 2) the percentages would be doubled – 16·0 per cent for contract A and 11·2 per cent for contract B.

15.5.1 DISADVANTAGES OF AVERAGE RATE OF RETURN

Although an improvement on payback, this method also has three weaknesses:

1 Like payback it fails to take account of the timing of receipts. It shows contract A to be the more profitable but fails to show contract B as the more liquid of the two. As is pointed out below, £1 in the pocket today is worth more than £1 tomorrow.
2 Annual fluctuations are smoothed out so that bad years are lost in the overall average.
3 The effect of taxation is ignored.

15.6 DISCOUNTED CASH FLOW METHODS

Quite clearly a more dynamic method than payback or average rate of return is required if investments are to be appraised sensibly, a method that will take care not only of total net cash flows and timing but also of the value of money. Discounted cash flow is such a method. This technique has two variants: the net present-value and the discounted-yield methods. It should be remembered that cash flow means the physical movement of cash both into and out of a business. The distinction between capital and revenue can be forgotten here as we are solely concerned with the flow of money.

15.6.1 THE TIME VALUE OF MONEY

It is a fact of life that money has a time value; £100 received today is worth more than £100 received at some future date. This is because money invested today (in a post office, a building society, the stock exchange, etc.) grows with time because of the interest factor. Therefore the longer the delay in receiving cash from a capital project the less attractive the sum becomes.

£100 invested today at 10 per cent would become £110 in one year (ignoring taxation and inflation), in two years £121, and so on, due to the effect of compounding. £100 today would be worth £110 in one year; conversely, £110 in one year from now at 10 per cent has a *present value* of £100. We have *discounted* £110 at 10 per cent over one year. Just as there are compound-interest tables for computing interest for any sum of money for any number of years, so there are *discount* tables for computing the *present value* of future incomes for any amount, time, and rate of interest.

Example:

Present-Value Tables

Year	9%	10%	11%	12%	13%	14%	15%	16%
1	0·917	0·909	0·901	0·893	0·885	0·877	0·870	0·862
2	0·842	0·826	0·812	0·797	0·783	0·770	0.756	0·743
3	0·772	0·751	0·731	0·712	0·693	0·675	0·658	0·641
4	0.708	0·683	0·659	0·638	0·613	0·592	0·572	0·552
5	0·650	0·621	0·593	0·567	0·543	0·519	0·497	0·476

It was said just now that £110 in one year from now discounted at 10 per cent has a present value of £100, because if £110 is multiplied by the discount factor under Year 1 at 10 per cent, we get:

$$£110 \times 0·909 = £100$$

15.6.2 NET PRESENT-VALUE METHOD

This method gives full weight to the importance of *timing*.

Example:
Suppose there are two projects involving alternative tipping contracts; each has a life of three years and requires a return of at least 10 per cent. Only one contract can be chosen. Both contracts have an initial outlay of £30,000 and an overall net cash flow of £40,000, as follows:

	Project A	Project B
	£	£
Capital outlay	30,000	30,000
Net cash flow: Year 1	7,000	6,000
Year 2	14,000	20,000
Year 3	19,000	14,000
	40,000	40,000

G

Discounting at 10 per cent we get:

		Project A		Project B	
Year	Discount factor	Net cash flow	Present value	Net cash flow	Present value
		£	£	£	£
0	1·000	30,000	(30,000)	30,000	(30,000)
1	0·909	7,000	6,363	6,000	5,454
2	0·826	14,000	11,564	20,000	16,520
3	0·751	19,000	14,269	14,000	10,514
		40,000	2,196	40,000	2,488

The present value of project B is higher than that of project A and it is therefore the one to choose. The reason for the higher present value of project B is that 65 per cent of the net cash flow is received in the first two years, compared with 52½ per cent for project A. This underlines the importance of the timing of receipts. Note also that the payback period of project B is shorter than that of project A (2.33 years compared to 2.56 years).

Notes:

1 The initial outlay of £30,000 is discounted at unity (1.000) because that is the present value of the outlay, and future net cash flows are discounted accordingly so that like values are compared with like.

2 The fact that each project has a *positive* net cash flow (*see* section 15.2) means that both will earn a return in *excess* of 10 per cent. Had the return been *nil* in each case it would mean that both projects would earn exactly 10 per cent in accordance with the discount factor. The last point is significant and brings us to the discounted-yield method.

15.6.3 DISCOUNTED-YIELD METHOD

The object of the yield method is to find the rate of interest at which the present value of income from a project is equal to the net cash outlay – in short, at which the net present value is zero (as described in Note 2 above). The rate which emerges from the exercise (which involves a series of trial-and-error computations) is then compared with some standard – either the desired rate of return or the cost of capital – to see whether the project is viable.

Example:

Suppose that the cost of capital for project B is 10 per cent and that we now wish to find the actual rate of interest or yield. In the table below we start with 10 per cent which is too low, the present value of income from the project being £2,488 over £30,000. We next try 15 per cent which is too high, the present value being below £30,000. We now try 14 per cent which is a little too low, the present value being just over £30,000. From this it can be deduced that the discounted rate of return is something more than 14 per cent. If we compare this with the cost of capital (10 per cent) we have a surplus of just over 4 per cent on the cash invested. The project is therefore viable.

Project B

Capital outlay: *£30,000*

	Net cash flow	Trial 1 (10%)		Trial 2 (15%)		Trial 3 (14%)	
		Discount factor	*Present value*	*Discount factor*	*Present value*	*Discount factor*	*Present value*
	£		£		£		£
Net cash flow							
Year 1	6,000	0·909	5,454	0·870	5,220	0·877	5,262
Year 2	20,000	0·826	16,520	0·756	15,120	0·770	15,400
Year 3	14,000	0·751	10,514	0·658	9,212	0·675	9,450
	40,000		32,488		29,552		30,112

Note on the Cost of Capital

We have glibly referred to the 'cost of capital' as though it were something easily determinable. Capital is made up of share capital, reserves, and loans, so the computation could be fairly complex, even for an average to be struck. Where short-term projects require short-term funding and a specific loan is obtained to cover the project, the exercise is that much easier.

15.6.4 EFFECT OF TAXATION

Taxation is very much a part of cash flow. Cash flow is enhanced by certain allowances and diminished through the payment of corporation tax. The taxes and allowances available in fleet operations are those already described in Chapter 14, namely: the first-year allowance, writing-down allowances, and corporation tax. These are at present 80 per cent, 25 per cent, and 40 per cent respectively.

In the following example it is assumed that both cash flows and allowances accrue at the end of each year, that corporation tax is payable on profit one year later, and that the tippers involved have no residual or scrap value at the end of either contract. The fact that there is a negative net present value of £355 supports the view that project B would earn a return on investment of something less than 14 per cent after tax (Note 2).

Example:

Project B

Year	A Cash flows	B Corporation tax (A × 40%)	C Tax allowances	D Tax saved by allowances (C × 40%)	E Tax payable (B − D)	F Cash flow after tax (A − E)	G Present-value factor (14%)	H Present value
	£	£	£	£	£	£		£
1	6,000	—	24,000	9,600	(9,600)	15,600	0·877	13,681
2	20,000	2,400	1,500	600	1,800	18,200	0·770	14,014
3	14,000	8,000	4,500	1,800	6,200	7,800	0·675	5,265
4	—	5,600	—	—	5,600	(5,600)	0·592	(3,315)
	40,000	16,000	30,000	12,000	4,000	36,000		29,645

less Capital outlay (30,000)

(355)

Notes:

1 Tax allowances:

		£
Year 1: First-year allowance (80% on £30,000)		24,000
Year 2: Annual writing-down allowance (25% on £6,000)		1,500
Year 3: Annual writing-down allowance (25% on £4,500)		1,125
Balancing allowance*		3,375
		30,000

* As the tippers have no scrap value there is a balancing allowance to cover the diminution in value.

2 The negative net present value of £355 shows that the return is less than 14 per cent. Discounting at 13 per cent we get:

Year	Cash flow after tax £	Present-value factor (13%)	Present value £
1	15,600	0·885	13,806
2	18,200	0·783	14,251
3	7,800	0·693	5,405
4	(5,600)	0·613	(3,433)
			30,029
	less Capital outlay		(30,000)
			29

The positive present value of £29 now suggests that the return is nearer 13 per cent than 14 per cent due to taxation. Management may therefore conclude that the return on investment will be just over 13 per cent.

15.6.5 LIMITATIONS OF DISCOUNTED CASH FLOW

The technique is limited in so far as a number of initial assumptions have to be made, namely:

1 'Life' of the project.
2 Forecast net cash flows which in some cases could extend for many years.
3 True cost of capital.

If the first assumption is wrong it will affect the second assumption which in turn will affect the overall result. Moreover, once a choice is made and a firm becomes committed, there is a tendency to let the project run its own course without testing whether or not the decision was a right one.

However, despite its limitations there is no doubt that discounted cash flow is probably the best method available, and if applied with caution and common sense it is a very useful management tool.

15.7 SUMMARY

1 The three methods of investment appraisal are based on payback, average rate of return on investment, and discounted cash flow (present-value and discounted-yield methods).

2 Discounted cash flow is the best method to use as it takes account of the present value of future net cash flows after taxation (both allowances and payments) and also reveals the payback period.

3 Discounted cash flow requires a considerable amount of forecasting, e.g. of capital cost, project life, annual expenditure and income, and the cost of capital. An error in forecasting could lead to a series of errors. Forecasting should therefore be of the highest quality.

4 Capital projects should not be left to run their own course once a decision has been made. Control information should be produced to see whether or not the decision was a right one in terms of cash flow and profit.

16 Management (Financial) Ratios

While this chapter will be of particular interest to transport companies (both own-account and haulage), the principles will nevertheless apply equally to those transport departments which operate on a self-accounting basis and to transport managers in general, as the financial health of a business is very much a part of dynamic management.

16.1 RATIOS AND THEIR USE

Management – or accounting or financial – ratios are obtained from a company's (or department's) set of accounts, which comprise the trading and profit-and-loss account, and the balance sheet which shows the company's assets and liabilities at a given date.

Ratios are used for two reasons:

1 To measure the financial position of a business at a given point in time.
2 To compare company performance with that of other companies within the same industry (known as 'interfirm comparison').

Although there are a number of universally accepted management ratios, discussion in this chapter has been restricted to the more important ones. Ratios can be divided into two types: *operating* (or profitability) ratios and *liquidity* (or solvency) ratios. Operating ratios are concerned with profit as a return on capital employed and on sales, and with sales/ capital employed. Liquidity ratios are concerned with the ability of staying solvent. Nowadays being solvent is just as important as being profitable; the two go hand in glove.

Example:

The figures overleaf relate to two companies and are used throughout this chapter for illustration purposes.

The first lesson to learn here is that company size is of no importance when computing and comparing ratios. Neither is it necessary to quote confidential figures such as turnover, profits, and assets in an interfirm-comparison scheme, as will be seen in section 16.6.

A.B. Carriers Ltd   *The Karry Co. Ltd*

Profit-and-Loss Statements (Year ending 19...)

	£	£	£	£
Turnover		61,000		270,000
less Direct costs		(46,900)		(197,000)
Gross profit		14,100		73,000
less Overheads		(12,520)		(67,000)
Net Profit		1,580		6,000

Balance Sheets (Date)

	£	£	£	£
Ordinary capital		20,000		50,000
Retained profit		4,500		7,000
10% debentures		12,000		10,000
Capital employed		36,500		67,000
Creditors	5,800		21,000	
Taxation	2,000		4,500	
Dividends due	2,000	9,800	7,500	33,000
		46,300		100,000
Buildings		12,000		20,500
Vehicles		21,000		31,700
Plant		2,000		2,500
Furniture, etc.		800		2,300
		35,800		57,000
Stock	2,000		8,000	
Debtors	8,000		31,000	
Bank	500	10,500	4,000	43,000
		46,300		100,000

The figures have been simplified but show at a glance that The Karry Co
Ltd is bigger than A.B. Carriers Ltd, with a higher turnover and tota
assets of £100,000.

16.2 OPERATING (OR PROFITABILITY) RATIOS

Operating performance is measured by three ratios:

1 Net profit/capital employed (%).
2 Net profit/sales (%).
3 Sales/capital employed.

16.2.1 NOTE ON CAPITAL EMPLOYED

Although 'capital employed' is traditionally defined as the sum of issue
share capital, reserves, and loans, there are other definitions, some of whic
are:

1 Total assets less current liabilities (i.e. issued share capital, reserve
loans, and future taxation).

2 Total assets less current liabilities but ignoring depreciation (i.e. fixed assets are included at cost).
3 Total assets less current liabilities but with assets revalued at current market prices.
4 Total assets at book values.
5 As 4 but ignoring depreciation.
6 As 4 but at market values.

To keep the matter as simple as possible, capital employed is here taken to mean the sum of issued share capital, reserves, and loans, even though the definition is by no means perfect.*

16.2.2 RETURN ON CAPITAL EMPLOYED

The desired return on capital is really made up of two amounts: the desired return on investment (perhaps a few per cent above the average money market rate), plus an additional sum to cover the risk factor of being in business. Whatever the desired rate the actual return must be measured. The formula is:

$$\frac{\text{Net profit}}{\text{Capital employed}} \times 100 = \text{R.O.C.E. (\%)}$$

The R.O.C.E. of A.B. Carriers Ltd is therefore:

$$£\frac{1{,}580}{36{,}500} \times 100 = 4.3\%$$

The ratio is calculated on net profit before taxation.

The return of 4·3 per cent is not strictly correct because debenture interest of £1,200 has been charged as an overhead expense against profit. To show a true return on the capital employed it is therefore necessary to add back the debenture interest, thus:

$$£\frac{2{,}780}{36{,}500} \times 100 = 7.6\%$$

16.2.3 RETURN ON SALES. The formula is:

$$\frac{\text{Net profit}}{\text{Sales (or turnover)}} \times 100 = \text{R.O.S. (\%)}$$

A.B. Carriers Ltd's R.O.S. is:

$$£\frac{1{,}580}{61{,}000} \times 100 = 2.6\%$$

* *See*, for example, R. G. Bassett, 'Return on Investment', *The Accountant*, Vol. 166, No. 5077, 6.4.72.

Thus for every £1 of sales a profit of 2·6p is made. The return would, of course, be affected by rates and volume fluctuations.

In this case there is no need to add back debenture interest.

16.2.4 CAPITAL TURNOVER

The ratio of sales to capital employed shows to what extent capital is being turned over. A.B. Carriers Ltd's ratio is:

$$\frac{\text{Sales (or turnover)}}{\text{Capital employed}} = £\frac{61,000}{36,500} = 1·6$$

Quite clearly the less capital needed per £1 of sales the more effectively capital is being employed. Indeed a number of operators have found on investigation that they could actually earn the same operating profit with less vehicles.

16.2.5 THE THREE RATIOS EQUATED

The last two ratios each form a constituent part of the first, as can be seen from the following equation:

$$\frac{\text{Net profit}}{\text{Capital employed}} = \frac{\text{Net profit}}{\text{Sales}} \times \frac{\text{Sales}}{\text{Capital employed}}$$

$$£\frac{1,580}{36,500} = £\frac{1,580}{61,000} \times £\frac{61,000}{36,500}$$

16.3 LIQUIDITY (OR SOLVENCY) RATIOS

It is stressed again that being liquid is just as important as making a profit, because unless a company can pay its employees and creditors on a regular basis the company will cease to operate. The ratios which enable a company to measure its liquidity position are the current ratios and the liquidity, acid-test, or quick ratio. Associated with these ratios is a third ratio: the debtors ratio.

16.3.1 CURRENT RATIO

This ratio measures the extent to which current assets cover current liabilities. In the case of A.B. Carriers Ltd the figures are:

$$\frac{\text{Current assets}}{\text{Current liabilities}} = £\frac{10,500}{9,800} = 1·07 \text{ to } 1$$

In short, if the current assets were realized for cash (i.e. stocks and debtors plus the bank balance) the total sum would more than cover the current liabilities and leave a balance of £700. The fact is, however, that the recommended current ratio in most companies is about 2. The above ratio falls short of this.

16.3.2 LIQUIDITY, ACID-TEST, OR QUICK RATIO

The real – or acid – test of liquidity is the ratio of quick assets to current liabilities, 'quick' referring to those assets which are quickly convertible into cash. Essentially these are cash and debtors *less* doubtful debts and cash discounts, if any.

Assuming that there are no doubtful debts or cash discounts the liquidity ratio of A.B. Carriers Ltd is:

$$\frac{\text{Quick assets}}{\text{Current liabilities}} = £\frac{8,500}{9,800} = 0.87 \text{ to } 1$$

This means that for every £1 liability there is only £0·87 to meet it at the date of the balance sheet. The recommended ratio is above 1.

16.3.3 DEBTORS RATIO

The ratio of debts to sales gives an indication of the average time it takes debtors to settle their debts, and is expressed:

$$\frac{\text{Debtors}}{\text{Sales (or turnover)}} \times 12 \text{ (or 365)}$$

A.B. Carriers Ltd's debtors ratio is:

$$£\frac{8,000}{61,000} \times 12 = 1.6 \text{ (months) (or } 7.62 \text{ to 1)}$$

In view of the company's low cash balance the ratio is not satisfactory and should be reduced to 1, i.e. one month's credit only (i.e. about £5,000).

16.4 SUMMARY OF RATIOS

A.B. Carriers Ltd's ratios may be summarized as follows:

Operating (or profitability) ratios
Return on capital employed 4·3%*
Return on sales   2·6%
Capital turnover   1·6
* (7·6% after adding bank loan interest)

Liquidity (or solvency) ratios

Current ratio	1·1
Quick ratio	0·9
Debtors ratio	1·6 (months)

Note that the ratios are as at the date of the balance sheet. Comparative figures for the previous year (or month) should be shown to reveal how the company is progressing.

16.5 INTERPRETATION OF RATIOS

Ratios by themselves mean little and should be compared with:

1 Average ratios for the industry or type of business.
2 Historical ratios to established trends.
3 Planned ratios to measure progress.

It should be the operator's aim to achieve above-average ratios.
    The ratios of A.B. Carriers Ltd reveal the following:

1 The company's profitability is poor: a mere 4·3 per cent on capital (after deducting debenture interest) before tax. The capital could have earned more had it been invested in a building society or an investment trust.
2 Capital turnover at 1·6 is poor.
3 The return on sales is poor: a mere 2·6p per £1 of sales. Questions should be asked about sales volume, traffic rates, and expenses.
4 Liquidity is poor: a ratio of less than 1. Questions should be asked about capital expenditure, the way in which vehicles are acquired and whether they are fully utilized, and whether there are vehicles surplus to requirements which could be sold to enhance the working-capital position.

16.5.1 REASONS FOR POOR RATIOS

A.B. Carriers Ltd's poor ratios could be due to a number of reasons. However, they all stem from a lack of effective management, without which no company can possibly survive.

(a) Poor profitability
    This can be due to a number of reasons, including:

1 Sales volume too low.
2 Rates too low.

3 Costs and overheads too high.
4 Poor utilization of vehicles.
5 Poor maintenance of vehicles.
6 Bad choice of vehicles.
7 Too many vehicles employed.
8 Lack of trained personnel.
9 Lack of business planning.
10 Poor customer relations.
11 Company badly organized.
12 Company badly sited.
13 Poor management.

(b) *Poor liquidity*

This can be due to:
1 Poor cash control.
2 Poor credit control.
3 Poor financial planning.
4 Lack of capital expenditure control.
5 Overheads too high.
6 Creditor payments made too soon.
7 Company under-capitalized.
8 Sales income too low.
9 Rates too low.
10 Poor budgetary control.
11 Poor management.

16.6 INTERFIRM COMPARISON

It is beneficial for firms within the same industry to compare company performance. Where, for example, one company is found to be below average there is obviously room for improvement in that company. Interfirm comparison can therefore act as a spur in improving management performance.

The basis of comparison in any interfirm-comparison scheme must always be the same if like is to be compared with like. Suppose that the directors of A.B. Carriers Ltd and The Karry Co. Ltd wished to compare the performance of their companies. The comparative figures would appear thus:

Operating ratios	*A.B. Carriers Ltd*	*The Karry Co. Ltd*
Return on capital employed	4·3 %*	9·0 %†
Return on sales	2·6 %	2·2 %
Capital turnover	1·6	4·0

(* 7·6 % before debenture interest)
(† 14·5 % before debenture interest)

	A.B. Carriers Ltd	*The Karry Co. Ltd*
Liquidity ratios		
Current ratios	1·1	1·2
Quick ratio	0·9	1·1
Debtors ratio	1·6	1·4

The conclusion to be drawn from these figures is that The Karry Co. Ltd is the better of the two companies. Its return on capital employed and capital turnover are both double that of A.B. Carriers Ltd, but the return per £1 of orders is lower at 2·2p. The Karry Co. Ltd is solvent at the date of the balance sheet (£1·10 covering every £1 liability) and its credit control is better than that of A.B. Carriers Ltd.

The directors of A.B. Carriers Ltd need to take a close look at their company, starting with themselves and the policies and objectives devised by them collectively. The items listed in section 16.5.1 should each be considered carefully and a positive plan of action should be implemented as quickly as possible.

By the same token, the directors of The Karry Co. Ltd should ask themselves why the return on sales is only 2·2 per cent and perhaps take a look at their rates structure.

16.7 OTHER RATIOS

The ratios shown are only some of the many ratios available. Other management ratios might include vehicle operating costs, warehouse, depot, and administrative expenses, and so on. The Centre for Interfirm Comparison uses many other ratios and has devised interfirm-comparison schemes for bulk liquid contractors, express carriers, and long-distance haulage and tipping vehicle operators, as well as a 'cost and productivity' scheme for the Road Haulage Association.

16.8 THE LIMITATIONS OF RATIOS

Ratios provide a good guide to company performance by comparing current performance with past or planned performance and with other companies' performance within the same industry. At the same time, ratios have their limitations. They do not, for example, take account of the changing values of money, nor of the present values of assets, while vehicles which are hired or leased are excluded altogether from ratio calculation. Moreover, interfirm comparison can only work where the accounting treatment is uniform and where companies are similar in the kind of work they do.

Ratios nevertheless provide a basic performance guide and encourage operators to become above-average performers.

16.9 SUMMARY

1 The purpose of analysing accounts is to determine company performance in terms of profitability and liquidity.

2 There are two types of ratios used to measure performance and financial health: *operating* (or profitability) ratios and *liquidity* (or solvency) ratios. The main operating ratios are expressed in the equation:

$$\frac{\text{Net Profit}}{\text{Capital employed}} = \frac{\text{Net Profit}}{\text{Sales}} \times \frac{\text{Sales}}{\text{Capital employed}}$$

The main liquidity ratio is the quick (or acid-test) ratio.

3 In computing ratios it is first necessary to define the meaning of 'capital employed' and other relevant terminology.

4 Interfirm comparison is a useful technique where similar companies within the same industry wish to compare performance, the object being to promote efficiency in those companies whose performance is below the average or accepted standard. It is essential that like is compared with like. The Centre for Interfirm Comparison operates a number of schemes for various sectors of the road transport industry.

5 Ratios provide a fair guide of a company's performance by comparing current performance with past or planned performance, and with that of other companies within the same industry.

6 Ratios have their limitations in that they do not take into account the changing values of money, the current value of assets, and leased or hired vehicles.

17 Financial Aspects of Business Planning

It is not within the scope of this book to deal with long-range (or corporate) planning. But a number of points arising from the long-range-planning process are pertinent here and provide a meaningful note on which to end: namely, planning for the future.

17.1 MANAGEMENT AND PLANNING

17.1.1 MANAGEMENT ACTIVITIES

It would be foolish to talk about planning without first having something to say about management, for unless management is aware of the purpose of its own existence there is little point in planning or doing anything. To quote a well-known phrase, a company is as good as its management; if a management is weak, the company is doomed to failure unless the right steps are swiftly taken to correct the situation.

The purpose of management can be summed up in its activities: planning, organizing, directing, and controlling, which include the motivation of staff.

1 *Planning* is the determination of the future activities of the whole or a part of a business in terms of its *objectives*, the resources it requires, and the way in which the resources are to be used.
2 *Organizing* is the acquisition and allocation of resources – namely manpower and fixed and current assets including money – as determined from planning.
3 *Directing* is ensuring that all the activities within the business operate cohesively and in sequence so as to achieve the objectives of planning.
4 *Controlling* is examining activities and the results of activities in the business to ensure that the objectives of planning are being achieved. Information gathered as a result of controlling is vital to the next phase of planning.

In other words, management exist to *achieve* the objectives of the company, but to do this the objectives must first be defined.

17.1.2 CORPORATE PURPOSE

Company objectives arise from a company's corporate purpose, which defines the type of business the company is in. As a policy statement the corporate purpose might read as follows: 'The company is engaged in the transportation of parcel deliveries, container freight services, bulk liquid services, and warehousing.' Once the reasons for the company's existence have been defined it is then a matter of deciding the objectives required to achieve the corporate purpose in terms of long-term profitability and growth (if that is the aim).

17.1.3 COMPANY OBJECTIVES

(a) Defining and quantifying objectives

Objectives must be defined and quantified. 'The company exists to make a profit' is not an objective; it is a subjective statement without meaning. To 'make a profit' it is first necessary to do certain things (e.g. acquire premises, vehicles, and working capital, penetrate the market, execute orders) and to relate profit to the overall capital investment that makes being in business possible. The amount of investment required depends, of course, on the planned scale of operations, which should be defined in a number of quantifiable objectives. These might be as follows.

Example:

1 *Market standing:* to increase the share of the market (defined under corporate purpose) as below:

(a) Parcel delivery services: by $x\%$ to $y\%$ in 19...
by $x\%$ to $y\%$ in 19...
by $x\%$ to $y\%$ in 19...
etc.

(b) Container freight services: by $x\%$ to $y\%$ in 19...
by $x\%$ to $y\%$ in 19...
by $x\%$ to $y\%$ in 19...
etc.

(c) Bulk liquid services: by $x\%$ to $y\%$ in 19...
by $x\%$ to $y\%$ in 19...
by $x\%$ to $y\%$ in 19...

(d) Warehousing services: by $x\%$ to $y\%$ in 19...
by $x\%$ to $y\%$ in 19...
etc.

Arising from 1:

2 *Rate of growth:* to increase company growth in terms of sales, profit, and net assets as follows:

(*a*) Sales (overall):	by $x\%$ over 19... in 19...
	by $x\%$ over 19... in 19...
	by $x\%$ over 19... in 19...
	etc.
(*b*) Profit before distributions:	by $x\%$ over 19... in 19...
	by $x\%$ over 19... in 19...
	by $x\%$ over 19... in 19...
	etc.
(*c*) Net assets:	by $x\%$ over 19... in 19...
	by $x\%$ over 19... in 19...
	by $x\%$ over 19... in 19...
	etc.
(*d*) Return on net assets:	$x\%$ 19...
	$x\%$ 19...
	$x\%$ 19...

Supporting figures for each individual sales mix would be detailed in the strategic operating schedules.

Arising from 2:

3 *Capital investment:* to finance operations as follows:

Year ended 19...: Existing capital plus retained profits.

Year ended 19...: Accumulated capital plus retained profits plus realization of quoted investments of £x.

Year ended 19...: Accumulated capital plus retained profits plus loan stock issue of £x.

Debt/equity ratio: x/y 19...
x/y 19...
x/y 19...

(*b*) *Planning strategies*

Once the broad objectives are defined – namely, market standing, rate of growth (i.e. sales, profit, and net assets), and the capital investment required to support it (including gearing ratios) – it remains to formulate a plan on paper as to the strategies to be employed. The plan should include the deployment of capital (i.e. acquisition of resources), assets, and personnel.

The plan should be drawn up by the chief executive with the full assistance and involvement of his senior managers, who alone will be responsible for its implementation and operation. Responsibilities for results can then be allocated and agreed. In short, each manager will agree with his subordinate (i.e. another manager or first-line supervisor) the goals to be achieved over the financial year.

(c) *Assessing managerial performance*

Objectives should be quantified in measurable terms such as money (profit, sales), ratios, time, percentages, etc., so that each manager's performance can be measured on a regular basis. Success may mean higher management potential or simply good luck as the result of external factors; failure may denote a training need or the influence of uncontrollable internal/external factors. Either way successes and failures should be analysed if managerial performance is to be truly measured. As it is the individual performance of each manager which contributes to company short-term (annual) goals and ultimately to the attainment of the long-term objectives, the importance of management development cannot be overstressed.

17.2 THE PLANNING PROCESS

In the above illustration a three-year plan was suggested. In practice this could be too short and a not unusual time scale is something of the order of five years and upwards, the first two years in detail, the remaining years in outline only. But however long or short the time span the important thing is to review the long-term business plan at least annually and update it if necessary. This ensures that the plan stays meaningful and capable of attainment.

The planning process varies from firm to firm. In the very large and complex company the plan needs to be very detailed, and is probably put together by a corporate planning department or committee. In the small to medium company the plan may be less sophisticated as the handful of managers who run the company will have the corporate objectives and short-term goals uppermost in their minds, although commitment on paper is still essential.

In general, most planning begins with sales – i.e. the present and planned share of the market – whether by the process outlined in F gure 35 or more simply by planning annual increments over a selected time span. But as sales must be expressed in money terms it is important to consider anticipated price rises and inflation, as these will affect the traffic rates.

For the planned sales – and therefore the planned return on capital – to be achieved, vehicles must be utilized efficiently. Vehicle capacity, availability (i.e. operating days), number of loads or drops, distances to be covered, route planning, etc. must all be carefully considered if operational planning is to mean anything. It might be discovered as the result of planning that additional tractors and trailers, and therefore drivers and garaging facilities, are needed if the sales/profit goals are to be met. This in turn will involve consideration of either the replacement of a number of existing vehicles with larger and more modern vehicles (thereby eliminating the need to increase costs by the employment of additional drivers) and the way in which they are to be financed, or the subcontracting of work to

Data	This year	19 _ _ _	19 _ _ _	19 _ _ _	19 _ _ _	19 _ _ _
Market total sales						
Planned share	%	%	%	%	%	%
Planned sales						
Present sales						
Sales gap						

1 The planned market share percentage might vary from year to year depending upon the resources available.
2 The difference between the planned-sales and the present-sales positions (extended over the years) gives the sales gap which has to be closed. How this is done would largely depend on company price and volume strategy, customer goodwill, innovation, diversification, and so on.
3 Where market sales for particular traffic is unobtainable it would be necessary to decide on the rate of growth over current sales, as explained in section 17.1.3(a) (2a).

FIGURE 35. Market-standing/sales plan.

other hauliers. (Another alternative would be the possible takeover of another but similar haulage company.)

The operating plan must include all the ancillary and supporting services which make a haulage business tick – suitable premises, workshops, depots, insurance, costing and accounting services, working capital, properly trained managers, supervisors, drivers, clerks, and operators – the whole being welded together in a cohesive business plan from which shareholders, employees, and customers will benefit.

Figures 36 and 37 show one method of displaying planning data in a general-haulage business. Figure 36 shows the financial plan for each year of the five-year plan, while Figure 37 shows the targets to be achieved over the same period.

It should be noted that the employment of budgetary control and standard costing (Chapters 11 and 12) will help to control costs. The employment of break-even analysis will help in the determination and maintenance of traffic rates (Chapter 13). The employment of cost comparison tables will help with the choice of vehicles (Chapter 14). While the employ-

		19___ £	19___ £	19___ £	19___ £	19___ £
1	Total sales	+				
2	Direct transport costs	−				
3	Gross surplus					
4	Administration	−				
5	Warehousing and storage	−				
6	Workshop (under-recovered)	−				
7	General	−				
8	Interest charges	−				
9	Pre-tax profit					
10	Taxation	−				
11	Net profit					
12	Land and buildings	+				
13	Trucks	+				
14	Motor cars	+				
15	Plant and equipment	+				
16	Office furniture and equipment	+				
17	Total depreciation	−				
18	Inventories	+				
19	Trade debtors	+				
20	Prepayments	+				
21	Cash and bank	+				
22	Creditors and accruals	−				
23	Taxation	−				
24	Dividends	−				
25	Net assets					
26	Ordinary share capital	+				
27	Preference share capital	+				
28	Capital reserves	+				
29	Revenue reserves	+				
30	Loans	+				
31	Other capital	+				
	Total capital					

(Table heading: A. HAULIER LTD — 5-YEAR FINANCIAL PLAN TO 19___)

FIGURE 36. Five-year financial-objective plan.

ment of investment appraisal techniques will help in appraising the viability of capital expenditure programmes, projects, and the like (Chapter 15).

After the course has been set for a business in terms of long-term

Target	19---	19---	19---	19---	19---
A. HAULIER LTD — 5-YEAR TARGET PLAN TO 19---					
1 Net profit/capital employed					
2 Net profit/sales					
3 Net profit/total assets					
4 Current ratio					
5 Quick ratio					
6 Debt/equity ratio					
7 Break-even sales					
8 km run					
9 tonnes carried					
10 Drops					
11 Operating days					
12 Vehicle capacity					
13 Utilization (%)					
14 No. of tractors					
15 No. of trailers					
16 Staffing: (a) Managers (b) Supervisors (c) Operatives (d) Office staff					
17 Growth (%): (a) Sales (b) Net profit (c) Total assets (d) Capital (e) Staff (f) Market share (g) Fleet					

FIGURE 37. Five-year target plan.

objectives and short-term goals, and the detailed short-term plans have been compiled and agreed, it remains to measure performance and take action when deviations emerge. Business planning should therefore be regarded for what it is: a sure and sound way of running a business which fully caters for change, innovation, and even diversification. The company that is prepared for change – by a swift updating of its business plan – is the one that survives when others go to the wall.

17.3 FINANCIAL PLANNING

Financial planning is an integral part of business planning and requires careful forethought if the right decisions are to be made. It determines the sources from which funds are to be raised to finance operations, and the way in which surplus funds are to be invested. Thus the employment of funds is made more efficient – which, after all, is what business and commerce is all about.

17.3.1 INTERNAL AND EXTERNAL FINANCING

Profit-and-loss statements, balance sheets, and cash flow statements covering the plan period make sense of planning in that they show business output in terms of net profit, return on capital, and assets. By the same token, capital planning is of importance because as a business grows (if that is the plan) and assets swell there must be a corresponding increase in the capital employed. (Remember the equation: capital + creditors = assets.) The growth in capital should therefore be planned and a debt/ equity ratio established.

It should first be considered whether the various types of funding are to be long- or short-term and obtained from internal or external sources. The answers very much depend upon the type of operation that requires financing. In general, short-term funding is often derived internally from retained profits, factoring (i.e. the sale of book debts to a factoring company), bank loans, or even depreciation and taxation provisions (providing there is cash to back them). Long- (or medium-) term loans are normally attracted from outside sources – shareholders or investment companies – although the sale and leaseback of premises is a mixture of internal/external financing.

17.3.2 DEBT/EQUITY RATIO

A look at a company's balance sheet will reveal whether all of the authorized share capital has been issued. If it has not then further shares could be sold for long-term investment purposes (e.g. a new depot, work-shop, or fleet of vehicles, or even a takeover on a share-and-cash basis).

Caution should be taken, however, with the further issue of ordinary shares; as these normally carry voting rights it could easily affect the future of the company if the shares were to fall into the wrong hands.

Consideration should therefore be given to the injection of debt capital (e.g. debentures), having regard to current interest rates, redemption date, and the anticipated return on investment. In this way voting powers are left unchanged and in good years the equity holders stand to gain, subject to dividend policy.

17.4 SUMMARY

1 Management activities comprise four main areas: planning, organizing, directing, and controlling which include the motivation of staff. Effective management therefore begins with planning and ends with the achievement of profit-orientated results.

2 Planning begins once corporate purpose and objectives have been clearly defined and quantified by the board of directors.

3 Planning should be the sole responsibility of the chief executive (gone are the figure-head days). He should be supported by the full involvement of his immediate subordinates who agree and implement the plan and assume their respective responsibilities for results on which they alone will be appraised.

4 Unless long-term objectives and short-term goals are quantified in measurable terms and responsibility for results is allocated and agreed down the management line, it will not be possible to effectively measure performance with a view to improving management and therefore business performance in the future.

5 The planning time scale and detail vary according to the size and complexity of a business.

6 Planning often leads to alternatives and therefore to full consideration of what is best for a company.

7 Business and management performance should be measured on a regular basis, the plan updated as situations change, and management training and development encouraged to improve future performance.

8 Financial planning is an integral part of business planning and determines the sources, internal or external, from which funds are to be raised to finance the business plan.

9 The debt/equity ratio should be carefully considered when attracting outside capital, having regard to voting powers, interest rates, and the anticipated return on investment.

10 The attraction of, use of, and company return on capital is what running a business is all about. Success can only come from realistic planning and sound management practice.

Reading List

Readers wishing to pursue the matters discussed in this book may find the following reading list helpful.

DISTRIBUTION MANAGEMENT

Physical Distribution Management, edited by Felix R. L. Wentworth (Gower Press, 1970).

Divided into five parts with twenty-seven chapters written by different specialists from the various distribution sectors, the book deals with the problems arising from distribution management, warehousing, bulk freight transport, delivery transport, and fleet management, and the ways in which different persons and firms have tackled them.

Planning A Distribution System, by Peter R. Attwood (Gower Press, 1971).

The emphasis here is on the word 'planning' as the book provides a very useful guide to setting up and controlling a complete distribution system. The book deals in some detail with strategic planning, market demand analysis, the siting of supply points, routeing and scheduling, and the ingredients of a successful distribution system. The text is supported by a number of useful illustrations. Recommended.

Distribution Management: Mathematical Modelling and Practical Analysis, by S. Eilon, C. D. T. Watson-Gandy, and N. Christofides (Griffin, 1971).

Essentially for readers who possess a sound working knowledge of mathematics. The book is a serious attempt to apply operational research techniques to the distribution function, and covers such topics as the number, size, and location of depots; vehicle scheduling and loading; fleet size; and the total cost function. A book of this nature naturally includes numerous computations, algorithms, and tables. A book for the OR man.

Computers in Vehicle Scheduling (The National Computing Centre Ltd, October 1969).

Describes the ways in which computers can be used to advantage in trip planning and thus reduce the overall transportation cost. The book is a summary of a survey carried out amongst companies involved in the transportation of goods, including the distributive trades, as well as organizations responsible for the development of computer programs, and outlines some of the systems available to the transport operator.

Croner's Road Transport Operation (Croner Publications Ltd).

An essential publication for every transport manager that deals with the legal aspects of goods vehicle operations both in the United Kingdom and the Continent of Europe. In loose-leaf form. Revised when changes take place.

The Transport Manager's Handbook, by David Lowe (Kogan Page, revised annually).

A useful handbook for all transport managers (and senior executives in transport companies) which deals with most aspects of transport legislation (e.g. Acts and Regulations, licences, drivers' hours, records, vehicle testing and plating, etc.).

Training for Transport and Physical Distribution, Department of Employment (HMSO, 1972).

This is 'A report by the Distribution and Transport Sub-Committee of the Joint Industrial Training Boards Committee for Commercial and Administrative Training'.

Broad-based recommendations of the sub-committee chaired by P. Haxby, Director of Training, RTITB, covering basic, general, and specialist training for those entering, or who require training in, the areas of transport and physical distribution. An ideal checklist for training personnel.

GENERAL MANAGEMENT

Principles of Management, by Henry L. Sisk (South-Western Publishing Co., 1969).

Books on general management are legion, but this is a particularly good one which adopts the systems approach to the management process. It deals in lucid detail with the management activities defined in Chapter 17: planning, organizing, directing, and controlling. A number of case problems are included, and the entire book makes good reading.

Improving Management Performance, by J. W. Humble (Management Publications, 1970).

Deals with the essential features and benefits of a management-by-objectives system. An excellent guide to launching MBO: setting objectives, measuring and appraising performance, organization and control.

Managing for Results, by Peter F. Drucker (Heinemann, 1964).

To achieve results the manager must be organized. The book deals with the economic tasks that any business has to discharge and organizes these tasks so that executives can perform them systematically, purposefully, and with understanding.

COST AND MANAGEMENT ACCOUNTING

Management Accounting by W. M. Harper (Macdonald and Evans: M & E Handbook Series, 1969).

An excellent introduction to the subject of management accounting. Although primarily designed for students the book will also appeal to readers who wish to understand the basic principles of the subject. It is clearly written and there are progress tests for those who require them.

Wheldon's Cost Accounting and Costing Methods, revised by L. W. J. Owler and J. L. Brown (Macdonald and Evans, 1960).

A basic and well-known textbook which takes the reader through most aspects of cost accounting.

Management Accountancy, by J. Batty (Macdonald and Evans, 1969).

Suitable for the mature manager who wishes to widen his knowledge of management accounting and the student sitting for one of the professional examinations.

Investment Appraisal, by A. L. Kingshott (Ford Business Library, 1967).

An excellent – but expensive – guide to investment appraisal techniques. Includes sections on variation and probability analysis, and numerous NPV tables (in need of revision at the time of writing), covering mainly plant and machinery and industrial buildings.

Discounted Cash Flow, by M. G. Wright (McGraw-Hill, 1967).

Examines the underlying concepts of DCF and shows that they can be readily understood at all levels of management and easily applied in making investment appraisal decisions. Recommended.

BUSINESS PLANNING

Introducing Corporate Planning, by D. E. Hussey (Pergamon Press, 1971).

A general introduction to corporate long-range planning. The book starts with the planning process and takes the reader through the setting of objectives, goals and standards of performance, corporate appraisal, financial, personnel, operating and market planning.

Business Planning for the Board, edited by Hugh Buckner (Gower Press, 1971).

An excellent guide which equips the director (and manager) with a concise and practical guide to planning procedures within the functional areas of finance, marketing, manpower, and product management. Planning mergers and acquisitions also included. Recommended.

Corporate Planning and the Role of the Management Accountant, I.C.M.A./ The Society for Long Range Planning, 1974.

A practical guide written and edited by experienced practitioners, offering advice on selected major areas of commercial and industrial activity. Not written specifically for management accountants, corporate planners, and the like, but for managers in general who are aware of the need for systematic analysis within their businesses.

Index

THE HEINEMANN
ACCOUNTANCY AND ADMINISTRATION SERIES

General Editor:
J. BATTY, D.Com.(S.A.), M.Com.(Dunelm), A.C.M.A.,
M.Inst.A.M., M.B.I.M.

ROAD TRANSPORT MANAGEMENT
AND ACCOUNTING